LOOKING FOR CONSENSUS?: CIVIL SOCIETY, SOCIAL MOVEMENTS AND CRISES FOR PUBLIC MANAGEMENT

CRITICAL PERSPECTIVES ON INTERNATIONAL PUBLIC SECTOR MANAGEMENT

Series Editors: John Diamond and Joyce Liddle

Recent Volume:

CRITICAL PERSPECTIVES ON INTERNATIONAL PUBLIC SECTOR MANAGEMENT VOLUME 2

LOOKING FOR CONSENSUS?: CIVIL SOCIETY, SOCIAL MOVEMENTS AND CRISES FOR PUBLIC MANAGEMENT

EDITED BY

JOHN DIAMOND

Edge Hill Business School, Edge Hill University, Ormskirk, UK

JOYCE LIDDLE

IMPGT Institute of Public Management and Territorial Governance, Aix-Marseilles Université, Aix en Provence, France

United Kingdom – North America – Japan
India – Malaysia – China

Emerald Group Publishing Limited
Howard House, Wagon Lane, Bingley BD16 1WA, UK

First edition 2013

British Library Cataloguing in Publication Data
A catalogue record for this book is available from the British Library

ISBN: 978-1-78190-724-5
ISSN: 2045-7944 (Series)

ISOQAR
REGISTERED
Certificate Number 1985
ISO 14001

ISOQAR certified Management System, awarded to Emerald for adherence to Environmental standard ISO 14001:2004.

INVESTOR IN PEOPLE

CONTENTS

PART TWO: CIVIL SOCIETY AND SOCIAL MOVEMENTS: CONSENSUS OR CRISIS?

PART THREE: REVIEW AND REFLECTION

LIST OF CONTRIBUTORS

Norjahan Begum	Teesside University, Middlesbrough, UK
Paul Bunyan	Edge Hill University, Ormskirk, Lancashire, UK
Graeme Chesters	International Centre for Participation Studies, Department of Peace Studies, University of Bradford, Bradford, UK
John Diamond	Centre for Local Policy Studies, Edge Hill University, Ormskirk, Lancashire, UK
Gary Hickey	Faculty of Health and Social Care and Education, Kingston University and St George's, Kingston Upon Thames, UK
Joyce Liddle	IMPGT Institute of Public Management and Territorial Governance, Aix-Marseilles Université, Aix en Provence, France
Michael Macaulay	Victoria University at Wellington, Pipitea Campus, Wellington, New Zealand
David McGuinness	Faculty of Engineering and Environment, Northumbria University, Newcastle upon Tyne, UK
Duncan McTavish	Public Policy and Management, Glasgow Caledonian University, Glasgow, Lanarkshire
Alyson Nicholds	Middlesex University Business School, London, UK
Simon Pemberton	School of Physical and Geographical Sciences, Keele University, UK

Lee Pugalis Newcastle Business School, Northumbria University, Newcastle upon Tyne, UK

Dina Wafa School of Global Affairs and Public Policy, The American University in Cairo, Cairo, Egypt

EDITORIAL ADVISORY BOARD

ACKNOWLEDGEMENTS

We would like to thank those who have contributed to this second volume in the series. We are, also, very appreciative of the support we have received from Emerald Group Publishing Limited and from our publisher – Tom Dark – who has been very patient with us both.

We welcome proposals to this series. Please contact the Editors via Emerald Group Publishing Limited.

INTRODUCTION: FROM AUSTERITY TO ACCEPTANCE?

SETTING THE SCENE

The collapse of the international banking system in the later parts of 2007 and through to the autumn (Fall) of 2008 has had a profound influence on the nature and content of public policy-making across North America and Europe. It is here that the language of the 'Age of Austerity' has meaning. While we cannot be sure of the long-term consequences of the choices made by elected politicians and the elites within the International Monetary Fund (IMF) and the European Union (EU), we can reflect on the immediate and medium-term impact of their decisions.

We are aware that in seeking to identify the short- to medium-term consequences of their policy choices we have to reflect too upon the responses from civil society institutions and organisations to the banking collapse. On the one hand, it seems to us, we can observe how political institutions of government (at all levels) accepted the need to adopt austerity measures. These institutional responses, while different in degree depending upon their remit and status shared a similar framework of analysis and interpretation, were rooted in a commitment to restore confidence in the banking system as quickly as possible. Thus, across Europe and North America, it was possible to observe a shared response to the global crisis.

At the risk of oversimplifying the political and public policy response we think that it contained four essential elements: first, there was a need to 'bail out' the banks so that they could be seen as financially secure (and while this did not result in the protection of all banks by the Fall of 2013 relative stability had been achieved); second, there was a requirement for cuts in public spending so that the bailouts could be 'afforded'; third, while there were attempts to develop a shared global response to the crisis, by early 2009 tensions within the IMF about the nature of the crisis included the concept of 'austerity' and marginalised alternative social and economic models as such alternatives emerged through 2009–2012.

We can map these elements to show how in the US and the UK it was difficult; and finally, the dominant discourse against the political and economic decisions taken within the EU and in the United States. It is this shared framework of analysis which we will explore later in this edited collection. We think that it illustrates the on-going instability present within the banking and financial system. In other words, while there appears to be an element of stability now across the Euro Zone, for example from the levels of crisis in Greece, Italy, Spain and Ireland back in 2011–12, the structures are still vulnerable and prone to bouts of crisis. Thus, nearly 6 years on from the visible crisis within the global banking system it is still fragile and 'at risk'. Indeed, it could be argued that as China begins to slip back in terms of economic growth the potential for crisis increases. The tensions within the EU (and especially the Euro Zone) and between the EU and the other global economic alliances or networks (e.g., the BRIC countries) are increasing too.

These crises are not just played out in differing economic contexts (the World Trade Organisation (WTO) attempts to secure agreements on the environment as well as seeking agreement on the activities of global companies from Google to Amazon and their tax commitments), they are present too in international political disputes. As well increasing tensions associated with the global banking crisis we can see also how political changes across North Africa and in the Middle East are also being shaped by the financial crisis and are shaping it too. The so-called 'Arab Spring' and its impact on Egypt is examined in this collection. We will return to it later in this chapter but it is important to comment that these processes (global financial instability and political crises) are linked. We think that in these responses across North Africa we can observe broader political movements of change.

These calls for political and social changes (however temporary they seem to outsiders) which were being played out in Egypt and Libya were also present on the streets of Madrid, Athens and Barcelona. The impact of the Occupy Now protests has been short-lived to some extent but may reveal a broader set of political and social developments. These developments form part of two separate chapters which follow. As they suggest the processes and developments they promote (and reflect) are more significant than any short-term response to the calls for austerity across different political and economic contexts.

The shared call for austerity which was made by the political elites from the US Congress and the Obama White House to the EU and the UK Coalition Government (elected in 2010) is striking in its degree of consistence. While there are areas of disagreement most significantly over the pace at which public spending needed to be cut there was a shared consensus that cuts were needed. At times over the past 2–3 years it has seemed as if these differences between elites within nation states and between the United States and the EU or the IMF were much more profound than they actually were.

Thus, although there were (and remain) quite marked areas of disagreement and within nation states themselves important localised political conflicts the broad consensus was that public spending as a proportion of GDP needed to be cut significantly. The 'big' picture within the advanced industrial economies of the North was one in which social and welfare services and spending was to be cut. As a consequence rising unemployment among public sector workers was set to rise and across these already depressed economies social and political instability was evident too.

The form this instability took varied and it is difficult to be precise about the extent to which there was a shared or common form of expression. The particular form it took differed from nation state to nation state. While we need to be cautious about claiming that there were shared or distinctive features to the growing political crises across the EU or within the United States we can observe certain characteristics which were present and those that might be described as 'absent'.

The 'present' characteristics were those that might be best seen in the Tea Party in the United States or in UKIP (United Kingdom Independence Party) in the United Kingdom. Both these political movements represented anti-elite or anti-establishment politics (although both in their separate ways have been supported by multinational companies or rich individuals as well as securing support from mass media organisations). They were able to lay claim to highly populist rhetoric in which they sought to represent the needs of the white working class or lower middle class voters who had 'suffered' through the economic collapse or were in opposition to what were seen as urban metropolitan politics. In the United States this meant direct opposition to Obama and what he was perceived to represent (urban, liberal, multi-racial politics and a commitment to health care reform). In the United Kingdom the space UKIP occupied was anti-EU membership, and a claim that the Conservatives (especially the leader David Cameron – the UK prime minister) had deserted its electoral base in favour of 'gay marriage' and High Speed 2 (the proposed rail link from London to the North West which was going to cut through many rural communities).

In both countries we can observe how electoral success (albeit it was short-lived in the case of the Tea Party) had a direct impact not just on national politics but local politics too. Both political parties might be described as 'social movements'. They were not conventional political organisations. They rejected (quite deliberately) some of the features of the mainstream political organisations in favour of a kind of 'anti-politics politics'. They were skilled at securing headlines and having an electoral impact too. In both countries we can see how the dominant parties moved to their frame of reference in order to counter their electoral appeal.

Within the Euro Zone and in some of the nation states which were not part of it there was a growth in the appeal of parties from the Far Right. The rise in support for parties which were close to or adherents of neo-Nazi ideas has been an important feature of this period. Across a number of countries – France, Greece, Hungary, the Netherlands and Austria – electoral support for these parties increased during this time. We need to be careful about what conclusions we draw from these developments. But the move to the Right was notable while support for the Left was not.

One of the interesting paradoxes of the banking collapse was the marked absence of significant support for those political parties of the orthodox left. In many ways it might have been anticipated that the scale of the collapse and the crises of capitalist economies across the world might have moved public opinion. It appears that the changes and movement of ideas were more subtle and nuanced.

CHANGES AND MOVEMENTS: ALL POLITICS IS LOCAL

We might reflect on the Age of Austerity as not so much the fault of the banking and finance sector but more the failings of those social democratic parties (in the United Kingdom – the Labour Party; in the United States – the Democratic Party and in differing EU countries – the Socialist Party (France) to regulate sufficiently and appropriately the banking sector. On one level we might assume that bankers and those working in the financial services industry might look to exploit loopholes in the regulations as they sought to maximise their profits. And across both the United States and the EU a shared development of the 1990s was the deregulation of the banking and finance sectors. In a sense, therefore, we might conclude that the shift in electoral support for parties of the Right was an inevitable outcome of the 'failings' of the social democratic left and centre.

However, such an observation may be too simplistic. While there have been these shifts in support as we have noted above there have been other political changes too at a local or city level, one of the most interesting and longer term developments of this period has involved two quite separate and different responses to the global financial uncertainty. In the United States and in Europe there has been the growth in small-scale direct action movements operating under the banner of 'Occupy Now'.

The form of protest they take is direct and specific. They organise to literally 'occupy' public spaces or buildings to highlight the ethical and political immorality of the banking collapse and its consequences. Their form of protest is short, direct and unconventional. It captures the interest of the media (although often not their support) and it provides a focus for a much more detailed and explicitly political and philosophical critique of the period running upto 2008 and beyond.

As is discussed below the 'Occupy Now' movement has its roots in the type of direct action which brought together activists and campaigners who protested against the WTO and the global political elites who meet under the banner of the G20. These very broad alliances of activists which are able to assemble quite diverse levels and groups of support from faith organisations and churches to green and environmental groups to the anti-Iraq war activists to the broad left of trade unions, peace movement and race, disability, gay and trade union organisations into a broad based oppositional movement were on the rise during 2010–13. They were, also, joined by those campaigning against the low corporate taxes paid by a number of global companies from Google to Amazon. Thus, while what these companies were doing was legal within those nations where they were registered it seems as if their payments represented an unethical response to the broader global crisis.

Occupy Now and those campaigns which highlighted the actions of global companies rather than just the decisions of elected politicians was one key shift in where the debate on the global financial crisis was being conducted. These campaigns were both global and local in their form. The internet and social media gave their message a global presence and connected actors and activists in ways that could not be imagined. As the cuts were being implemented within member states of the Euro Zone street level protests increased. Across Spain and Greece opposition to the cuts included the usual forms of expression: street-based demonstrations organised by the trade union movement. But increasingly we could observe how the 'traditional' trade union leadership across Europe was unprepared for the political response at the city or neighbourhood level. In Barcelona and Madrid and Athens long after the formal demonstrations had been completed demonstrators remained to protest and to occupy the streets.

These localised activities were, often, outside the control of the leadership of the trade unions or the mainstream parties. One of the consequences of the scale and depth of the cuts in social and welfare spending was the increase in levels of poverty, dependence on charities or the churches for food and support and an alienation from the traditional forms of organisation. In the United Kingdom the incoming Coalition Government sought to harness the skills and imagination of a large and diverse voluntary and community sector or NGO community. The vision for David Cameron was transforming the United Kingdom into a 'Big Society' in which the charitable/voluntary sector replaced the state as a provider of welfare and social/health services. The means to achieve this ambition was to be found in the creation of an army of 'community organisers'. We discuss what happened to this initiative below.

But it is important to note how these developments – street level opposition to national and local elites; broad base coalitions being created in which traditional parties of the left were marginal; innovative forms of protest which captured the popular imagination; and the use of social media to promote ideas and protest – were being caught and used in North Africa.

The so-called 'Arab Spring' can be seen to both enthuse and be enthused by these street level protests. As is explored below the rise of the Arab Spring, especially, in Egypt has a number of serious and unintended consequences. In this section we want to highlight two key messages (for us) of the profound and transformative events in Cairo and across North Africa.

The first key element to identify is the inability of the Western leadership (in the United States or Europe) to influence or control events. The significance for us of what happened is its speed and scale. And the second is the ways in which in such situations conventional politics and political institutions are (or are not) able to be absorbed into the new arrangements or they are swept aside.

It is this 'new' politics which we think is significant for those engaged with the disciplines or fields of study of public management or public administration. The global collapse of the banking and financial sectors had a profound impact on political institutions and systems around the world. We recognise that we are living and working in times of transition and change. The instabilities in the institutional architecture of the northern advanced industrial economies are likely to remain for some time to come. We anticipate that the changes within nation states across Europe and North America are likely to take some time to settle. The challenge is, in part, to understand or to interpret the trends and developments in political structures and forms of governance at all levels of the state which the crises of 2007–08 have stimulated.

The response to the cuts in welfare spending across Europe and North America appears to have taken the form of a wish to return to the status quo. Trade unions and local community groups in different cities and urban areas appear to have adopted a politics of a 'return to the pre-2008 world'. Their rejection of the cuts in social and welfare spending and a desire to see a counter-narrative to the one promoted by neo-liberalism of welfare spending or infrastructure investment acting as a stimulus to economic growth is not shared by political elites.

The new conventional wisdom of the UK Coalition and its Labour opposition as well as centre-left governments in the EU is that cuts in public spending are a reality which have to be adjusted to. In North America, despite growth in the economy, the Obama White House remains weakened in its relationship with Congress and he is already seen as a 'lame duck' president.

It is at the local level that we think we can see a more fluid set of conditions. At the level of city hall or the region it is possible to see a much more complex set of relationships being enacted. There are three sites of interest here we think to examine and to reflect on.

First, there is the nature of the local alliances and networks which make up local political elites at the neighbourhood or ward or city level. The relationship between elected councillors, appointed officers or professional staff and voters/residents is (in part) shaped by the decisions made to invest or to allocate resources into particular places or initiatives.

We want to draw on the experiences of urban regeneration initiatives as a way into understanding and analysing these relationships. There are two chapters described below which do precisely this. They examine different facets of UK urban regeneration processes and in so doing it is possible to identify different sets of relationships, power structures and decision-making systems present in such initiatives. These complex inter-relationships, also, shape policy-making at a different scale of decision-making. At a level above the city or the neighbourhood the regional scale (with all its limitations) provides an important point of reference and analysis.

Within these local political elites we can see tensions and difficulties with the decision made centrally. Whether in the United Kingdom, the EU or the United States local party loyalties in times of such economic crisis cannot be assumed. Indeed, one of the features of the forms of governance and accountability favoured in the United Kingdom and the

United States is one which devolves decision-making down to quasi-independent boards or management committees (e.g. for providing health care, public housing or education). These independent boards with elected political figures or political leaders appointed to them do have local loyalties. They are part of the local/city elites with a expressed sense of commitment to their geographic community. As the cuts deepen we can expect to see these loyalties tested.

Second, we think that the roles, responsibilities and actions of public managers need to be examined and understood. The nature of the present crisis suggests that there is a crisis too for those involved in the professional leadership of local areas and services. In a very narrow sense we can see that such public professionals (across a range of different disciplines) did not enter their areas in order to cut services in the ways in which they are being asked/required to do. We might expect, for example, to see indicators of resistance from such public professionals. These might range from outright opposition leading to resignation to not applying for senior posts (in the United Kingdom, for example, there is a crisis in the low levels of application for heads of schools) or to encouraging resistance through professional bodies or trade unions.

The nature of the present crisis does represent a very direct challenge to received ideas of what constitutes a public manager, their roles and expectations, as well as their obligations and responsibilities. We think that the scale and depth of the crisis have very serious implications for the professional development, learning and status of public mangers as a profession.

Indeed we can observe how despite the different political, social and professional traditions associated with public management and public administration across Europe (including the accession countries to the EU) and North America there are some key shared assumptions and expectations. These shared assumptions are directly linked to the scale of the economic crisis. The 'Age of Austerity' is as much a crisis for the discipline and practice of public management as it is for politicians and residents.

Third, we think that we can learn about the short-term (and possible long-term) impact of the crisis by looking at the nature and process of local politics and the relationships between the politics of campaigning and social change to the administration of services.

We anticipate that by drawing together the literature on some of the social movements which have emerged since 2008 – Occupy Now, Community Organising and the Arab Spring – we can begin to analyse their impact on decision-making at the local level.

As the chapter on the Arab Spring describes the politics of change and radical reform on the streets of Cairo had a direct impact on those who developed and managed the programmes of public management or administration based in the University.

The scale and (perhaps) diffused nature of Occupy Now might have less direct impact in the short term on decision-making at a city level but it might be part of a broader process of change for younger activists and community leaders. These social movements open up a way into examining leadership networks outside the existing systems and structures. They provide another way into how we think of 'leadership' models and decision-making processes. In these particular examples they do sit in opposition to liberal democratic ideas of representative leadership – accountable to a clear constituency. For public managers (in times of crisis) we think that such more devolved and decentralised models of leadership and decision-making are much more of a challenge. They add to the prevailing sense of instability and uncertainty.

STRUCTURE OF THE COLLECTION

In bringing together these different contributions we have tried to group them according to our framework for analysis. There are a number of contributions which quite explicitly examine the overview to the crisis. In his chapter Duncan McTavish provides a series of insights and reflections on the global nature of the crisis and reminds us of how we got here; Dina Wafa, Graeme Chesters and Paul Bunyan put the politics of opposition and resistance into context. They draw on their research to reflect on the Arab Spring – Dina writes from her direct experience of designing programmes of management and governance for a new audience, Graeme looks at the international impact of the Occupy Now movement and Paul analyses the underlying conceptual framework for the Community Organising initiative in the United Kingdom.

Simon Pemberton and Alyson Nicholds in their separate chapters examine the impact of regeneration and regional programmes on how we frame local decision-making and open up such processes to community participation and engagement.

Both Michael Macaulay and his colleagues together with Lee Pugalis and David McGuinness offer different but, we think, complementary analyses. Michael's work and those of his colleagues consider the ways in which we might reflect upon concepts of governance, integrity and ethical decision-making in the context we find ourselves. Their work looks at (and reflects upon) the shift in the United Kingdom and elsewhere to develop standards and frameworks for decision-makers and political leaders.

Lee Pugalis and David McGuinness explore the ways in which we might make sense of how poor or deprived communities might work through the global impact of the Age of Austerity. Their work sits well with the chapters by the other contributors to this collection because they provide a different lens through which we might think about these relationships and changes.

Over the past 30–40 years the concept of 'urban regeneration' while it can be contested and challenged has become the label under which neo-liberal models of economic development linked to the needs of the private sector have been dominant. Social models of regeneration which have focused on meeting the needs of communities or places where there is economic decline and disinvestment have become less recognised.

These tensions and difficulties of resolving policy or political differences have, we suggest, in different places shifted from being heard in parliaments or assemblies to the streets. The social, economic and policy crises of 2008 have become political. They are not some temporary shift or mood change, we think they illustrate the nature of the long-term changes we are part of. This collection provides a set of insights, reflections and analyses to enable us to imagine the medium- to long-term consequences of what these changes might mean.

John Diamond
Joyce Liddle
Editors

PART ONE

THE PUBLIC POLICY CONTEXT: INTERNATIONAL TRENDS

These chapters examine different aspects of contemporary public policy and public management thinking. In their different approaches they explore shared themes of the national and global crisis of confidence in institutions of governance and decision-making; the impact of the failure of the regulatory agencies and national governments to anticipate the banking and finance crises; the scale and reach of the crises over time and space and the different ways in which the crisis is experienced in nation states; the response of national governments and agencies to the crisis and the extent to which there remains a real and fundamental crisis of confidence in liberal democratic institutions; and the nature of the response to these crises across nation states and the challenges these create for managers and practitioners.

In this section of the collection we wanted to capture the depth of the crises and also to think about different aspects or elements of it. These chapters do look at these broad conceptual and policy-related issues. In doing so they frame an on-going research and enquiry agenda which we hope will be reflected in subsequent volumes of this series.

'WHO'S RESPONSIBLE FOR THE STATE WE'RE IN?' GOVERNMENT AND PUBLIC SECTOR: ACCOUNTABILITY AND RESPONSIBILITY IN AN ERA OF CRISIS AND AUSTERITY

Duncan McTavish

ABSTRACT

Purpose – *To explore the shifting contours of politico-economic governmental responsibility and accountability from the consensually driven Keynesian welfare state model through to the market focused neo-liberal new public management (NPM) approach and beyond. In particular the chapter addresses the post-2008 crisis and austerity environment. It questions why the apparent failure of the market privileged neo-liberal model resulting in financial crisis and the prolonged aftermath has not led to an alternative recognizably coherent or consensually based approach to government and state responsibility for politico-economic management, and the implications of this for the accountability of public services.*

Looking for Consensus?: Civil Society, Social Movements and Crises for Public Management
Critical Perspectives on International Public Sector Management, Volume 2, 3–23

ISSN: 2045-7944/doi:10.1108/S2045-7944(2013)0000002002

Methodology – *The chapter draws on extensive literature across economic, social policy, public management and other fields as well as government and key institutional documents and reports. This enables a comparative perspective on governmental approaches to politico-economic management and management of public services, addressing key areas of consensus, responsibility and accountability.*

Findings – *The chapter traces the trajectory of governmental accountability and responsibility from Keynesianism to neo-liberalism and NPM, conceptually grounding these policy shifts and punctuations. It suggests that the key issue – why the dramatic failure of the neo-liberal model from 2008 has not led to a new emerging paradigm – may be answered not simply by reference to the continuation of neo-liberal approaches, but by appreciating that a number of countries have in fact implemented adaptive and resilient systems which have accommodated many of the neo-liberal NPM prescriptions. The findings conclude with some speculation on the future of government and public sector accountabilities and responsibilities.*

Keywords: Accountability; adaptive resilience; austerity; consensus; neo-liberalism; NPM; responsibility

INTRODUCTION

Accountability, Responsibility and the Post-1945 Consensus

There is a common understanding of a post-1945 paradigm with regard to the responsibility of the state for economic management and the delivery of (an increasing range of) public services. Underpinning policy prescriptions were based on Keynesian economics, itself developed as a response to the 1930s' economic depression and mass unemployment. At the heart of this was a welfare state with a commitment to low unemployment, steady economic growth and the use of fiscal and other powers to regulate demand (i.e. increasing demand when recession or low growth was evident, reducing demand when inflation threatened) to achieve these ends (Grant & Wilson, 2012). This was based on a political settlement including social safety nets, pensions, some socialized public services, a range of redistributional policies and a growth in the range of public services available to the citizenry at large with increased access not only to security, health and safety net services but also to services expanded on the basis of improving social mobility and life-enhancing opportunities for a broader range of social groups through, e.g., the expansion of post-school and higher education) (Crouch, 2011). This approach however should not be considered monolithic or without significant nuance. There were variations in European experience: social partners in some Scandinavian countries were much more closely engaged with economic and welfare policy delivery; in Germany, the more systemic involvement of organized labour, employers and financial institutions (Crafts & Torlino, 2008); the United States provided a somewhat different model, with some political, ideological and intellectual hostility to Keynesianism (Skidelsky, 2009; Weir, 1989), but a form of welfare Keynesianism did exist with governments accepting responsibility for some subsidized health care and the creation of Medicare and Medicaid (Grant & Wilson, 2012) – indeed with President Nixon stating in 1970, 'I am now a Keynesian in economics' (cited in Grant & Wilson, 2012, p. 3).

In parallel, in Europe though to a lesser extent in the United States, socio-political coherence and cohesion was underpinned by government assuming responsibility and accountability for a range of public service provision. No more so than in Britain, where the first cabinet minister with responsibility for the National Health Service, Aneurin Bevan famously said that if a bed pan is dropped in a ward in Tredegar (in Bevan's Wales), the noise of it should be heard in Westminster (cited in Klein, 1995). Large voter turnout, (in the main) consensus politics despite party competition (in Britain termed Butskellism after a leading 'leftish' Conservative minister RA Butler, and the 'rightish' leader of the Labour Party Hugh Gaitskill), indicated an environment of political (democratic) accountability and legitimacy. Indeed in many countries there was continuous intervention by government to maintain economic fine-tuning at any sign of political disquiet which might unsettle these arrangements (over, e.g., rising unemployment) (Massey & Pyper, 2005).

The accountability-responsibility configuration of government thus described has various features. This is best depicted as hierarchical ordering of governmental activity and service provision through mono-organizational bureaucracies structured on Weberian type principles, with relatively direct governmental control, ultimately the responsibility of directly elected politicians. As far as service provision goes, citizens are clients with little say about services which are largely professionally dominated. So, hierarchies and public servants are dominant (Hartley, 2005). Traditional public administration has been stylized as

- dominated by bureaucracy;
- hierarchical and function based;
- separation of roles between non-partisan officials and political leadership;
- use of procedures and processes;
- monopoly of provision by public organizations;
- in the public interest;
- hierarchical chain of reporting and accounting;
- administrative tasks, instruction based, little emphasis on personal responsibility.

(Burnham & Horton, 2013; Hughes, 2012; Kickert, 1997)

POLICY PUNCTUATION POST-1970S FROM GOVERNMENTS AND BUREAUCRATS TO MARKETS, CONTRACTS AND PERFORMANCE

There were significant changes (internationally) in the external environment from the mid-1970s, stressing the post-1945 paradigm, which in turn brought on to the political and policy agenda shifting expectations of the role of the state. From the early 1970s there was a sustained slowing down of economic growth triggered by the sharp rise in oil prices after 1973. Kreiger (1986) estimated that compared with the previous 10 year period, 1973–1981 saw a significant reduction in the average increase in world trade from 9% to 3%. This created fiscal pressures and led to a difficult environment for government-initiated expenditures. The operation of what has been called the Keynesian welfare state presented policy-makers with a dilemma. The political pressure to maintain social and other public expenditures, and high levels of employment, made it difficult in periods of reduced economic growth to use the fiscal and other levers to control inflation, leading to stagnation and inflationary pressures in the economy – stagflation. Politico-economic responses to this seemed to indicate an inability of the existing policy paradigm with its foundational premises on the roles and responsibilities of government to simultaneously maintain and sustain public expenditure, high employment and stable (low) inflation. For example, the attempt by governments to maintain high levels of employment without inflationary pressures led to wage control initiatives. The associated attempt to work collaboratively with organised labour was in some countries for a time relatively successful (e.g. Austria and [West]

Germany), but in others not. For example in the United Kingdom the attempt was not successful, there the perception being that trade unions were over-powerful, obstructive and indicative of the failure of the system to cope (Grant & Wilson, 2012).

An alternative intellectual and policy paradigm was applied to address this. Reagan and Thatcher inspired approaches (typified by Reagan's inaugural address in 1981, 'in this present crisis, government is not the solution to our problem; government is the problem') had a conceptual underpinning. According to figures and thinkers like Niskanen (1971, 1973, 1994), Hayek's (1944) – the former served on Reagan's Council of Economic Advisers – individual choice was superior to bureaucratic mandate and also more efficient since it was based on market incentives. Public choice theory was based on the assumption that bureaucrats act rationally (as in classical economic theory) to maximize their own interest; according to this view public organizations make a case for increased budgets leading to an oversupply of service, not easily challenged by the political system. This provided a convenient explanation of the pre-existing Keynesian-based system's apparent failure: its reliance on public expenditures via fiscal and economic management led to bureaucratic and state overload.

Much of this foundational thinking has influenced, been adapted, pragmatized as well as popularized to form a rationale for doctrines of new public management (NPM). Osborne and Gaebler's 'entrepreneurial government' has focused on inter alia competition between providers; empowerment of citizens and communities (i.e. at the expense of the state and government); customer choice; earning not just spending money; and market rather than bureaucratic mechanisms (Osborne & Gaebler, 1992). NPM approaches have been adopted in most OECD (and other) countries, though the scope and impact have varied. Osborne and Gaebler's approach was openly adopted by US Vice President Gore in the National Performance Review in 1993 (Van Dooren, Bouckaert, & Halligan, 2010). The idea of a small state was a key driver for many (Hughes, 2012); New Zealand and the United Kingdom were particularly driven. Countries with a more individualist, rather than a collective culture have tended to be in the forefront (e.g. the United States, the United Kingdom, Australia in the former, Finland and Germany in the latter), as have those with an administrative culture (in terms of parliamentary and political sovereignty like the United Kingdom, New Zealand and Australia) vis-à-vis those more aligned with legal constitutionality (e.g. many continental European countries). The strength of the policy advice system to ministers is also important –

those with greater accentuation on business and managerial advice as more receptive than those being advised from a different or more diverse community. Also significant is the representative system, with majoritarian and centralized systems (like the United Kingdom) often able to drive radical change more easily than less centralized or bicameral or systems prone to gridlock (like the United States) (for a comprehensive account, see Kickert, 2003; Pollitt, 2007; Pollitt & Bouckaert, 2004).

Drawing on OECD survey material (Peters, 2012), there has been a variety of policy responses to economic management and public – private interactions. In the period 1990–2007, all OECD governments except Germany changed budgeting, administration, employment, operation and public sector collective bargaining arrangements (OECD, 2005; Pollitt & Bouckaert, 2004). In many countries, reducing or re-allocating public expenditure was considered a national priority and implemented top-down. Many North American and European countries in the name of NPM decentralized public sector pay bargaining structures, introduced performance-related pay, individualized bonuses and grew part-time and temporary contracted employment (OECD, 2008; Peters, 2012). In other countries another approach was followed (e.g. Sweden, Germany and Austria): multi-level collective bargaining was implemented where budget cuts were negotiated centrally but private providers or local or regional tiers of government cut costs by managing, for example, pay flexibly; in some countries contracts were operated on a part-time or flexible basis below the nationally collectively bargained rates (Hall, 2005). Other practices included privatizations, contracting out and purchaser-provider splits to create a market where none existed previously (e.g. in the UK National Health Service – Pollock, Leys, & Price, 2005).

Despite such variety, governments converged substantially over the period 1990–2005, introducing fiscal austerity measures and changing public sector management in line with NPM principles through privatization, marketization and public–private partnerships (Peters, 2012). It makes sense to talk of the years from the 1980s in terms of a 'neo-liberal consensus'. In fact we can go further and state that internationally the acceptance of reliance on market forces to steer economic development, the preference for private provision of goods and services, have been accepted as tokens of good governance, propagated by international bodies like the World Bank, International Monetary Fund (IMF); this is generally known as the Washington Consensus (Wilson, 2012).

We are therefore talking of a new paradigm from that existing between 1945 and the late 1970s. Punctuated equilibrium is a useful conceptual lens here. This was understood in terms of an existing policy monopoly – the policy founded on Keynesianism with an accompanying institutional structure able to implement and deliver – or certainly if not a monopoly, a broad practice consensus. This was re-inforced by a policy image (i.e. the policy was understood, communicated and mediated in terms of the powerful idea of the desirability and ability to maintain high levels of employment, acceptable levels of inflation etc.) (Baumgartner & Jones, 1993). This policy was maintained in equilibrium by the coalition of supporting interests, for example neo-corporatist interests like trade unions and employer organizations, political interests (elected representatives and other groups), insider communities like civil servants and other parts of government machinery. This equilibrium and policy monopoly was effectively punctuated and discontinued due to the changed political and economic environment emanating from around the mid-1970s. Economic downturn and significant levels of inflation forced by soaring oil prices led to attempts at maintaining the core Keynesian prescriptions, but the need to control inflation through wage controls was unpalatable to some key policy actors (especially trade unions) resulting in a loss of consensus; added to the perception of an overloaded state and the emergence of alternative ideological and policy prescriptions, neither the policy monopoly nor a re-enforcing policy image were sustainable. Arguably what emerged from the 1980s was a broad policy monopoly around a neo-liberal world view, notions of how government responsibilities should be constructed and how government and public services should run (along the principles of NPM). Although, rarely used in such a broad macro context, punctuated equilibrium and policy monopoly are useful analytical frameworks, but we should be aware of some nuance and qualification. First, there are a variety of NPM approaches used in different countries and settings, so international policy monopoly is a rather broad concept without detailed assessment. Second, the configuration of policy actors and how they play out their actions and interests varies: for example the role of social partners is well developed in some European and Scandinavian countries, but much less so in the United Kingdom and the United States. Third, there are various points of contestation in this policy arena, perhaps over-stretching the term monopoly. Fourth, the creation of a new policy monopoly (which it is suggested the neo-liberal, NPM paradigm is) as currently understood indicates that the previous monopoly could not be sustained (i.e. was unsuccessful) because participants could not insulate decisions from a wider audience, leading to competition for access to government resulting in political instability caused by group conflict (Jordan & Maloney, 1997). Notwithstanding, it could be argued that many of the actors (e.g. some policy communities) are essentially the same, are constant over a long time period; in fact it's not about a new audience as such, just that some actors are increasingly privileged over others (e.g. those pro-business or pro-market) or that interests become somewhat more fragmented across looser networks. Nonetheless, this framework is useful to conceptualize understanding. Aspects of the Washington Consensus can appear to crowd out alternative policy prescriptions, and there does appear at times to be a supporting policy image portrayed through a range of institutions like the IMF, World Bank, G8 etc. There is undoubtedly a fruitful and under-exploited research field here to complement and accompany the traditional and now classic policy sector or national government-based studies (e.g. Baumgartner & Jones, 1993; Heclo, 1978; Jordan, 1981), and the interesting range of work on policy ideas debating the extent to which policy paradigms and images are strongly influenced by the material interests of certain actors or whether the underlying images and ideas themselves have more privileged standing (Beland & Cox, 2013).

The post-1980s environment also saw a conceptually linked shift in the delivery and accountability arrangements for public service provision. A 'traditional' model of public administration and management with a focus on vertical line management in (mainly) mono-organizational bureaucracies (termed by some as statist and bureaucratic, e.g. Hartley, 2005; Osborne, 2006) with the lodestone of accountability for the use of mandated public funds was transformed into one structured around NPM principles, a concomitant of a changing macro politico-economic paradigm as indicated. Accountability arrangements under this model are similar in the sense of ultimate accountability for the use of public funds continuing to be of fundamental importance – and indeed there is a rich body of literature which highlights the continuing role of traditional accountability mechanisms via statist and bureaucratic instruments, through the varying developments in approaches to public service delivery (see, e.g., Fenwick, Miller, & McTavish, 2012); however markets, competition, contracts and accompanying organizational practices are key components of how accountability is defined and practiced. In addition the fragmentation implied in the NPM approach (where a number of organizations may be involved in delivery chains) often necessitates forms of co-ordination or layers of reporting in the accountability process. The contrasts in the traditional and NPM models can be summarized (Table 1).

Table 1. Traditional and NPM Models of Public Service Delivery.

	Traditional Model	New Public Management
Underlying principle	State bureaucracies	Markets and competition
Delivery of public services	Hierarchy and bureaucratic principles; unified chains of command; management by instruction, regulation and task definition	Contracts arranged on market or cost-based principles; creation of markets/competition internally if externalization not available; service level agreements
Accountability	Hierarchies and mono-organizational boundaries; accountability to mandating bodies (e.g. government departments)	Performance management arrangements; contractual compliance; accountability to mandating bodies often via intermediaries (e.g. NDPBs, arms length bodies, inspection frameworks)

Source: Adapted from information in Kickert (1997); Kelly et al. (2002); Hughes (2012); Burnham and Horton (2013).

THE DOWNFALL NEO-LIBERAL FAILURE

The financial crisis and ensuing austerity could perhaps have been expected to lead to a policy and paradigmatic shift from the neo-liberal market-based thinking in the sense that this model of politico-economic organization had palpably failed. It is beyond the scope of this chapter to analyse in depth the factors surrounding this failure; however a brief contextual analysis is important for the chapter's overall organizing theme.

The defaults on subprime mortgage loans (accelerating from 2007) and the collapse of Lehman Brothers in 2008 triggered systemic failure and near collapse of the global financial system (Reich, 2008; Tett, 2010). This crisis had its genesis in the neo-liberal model. The liberalization of first domestic and then international capital markets led to an explosion of securitized financial products and instruments, based on a rupturing of traditional methods of intermediation (i.e. buying and selling of products through known channels or brokers) and a proliferation of financial products and instruments based on the packaging, trading and distribution of, for example, credit default swaps, collateralized debt obligations, insurance backed products; many of these were based on an assumption of continuing rising asset (often property based) prices, thereby creating a 'sell on' market (Posner, 2009). In short, the system was internationally integrated, somewhat volatile and exposed to decline in asset prices. The low interest rate environment heralded by the US Federal Reserve in the early 2000s and followed in Europe meant that in many economies these low interest rates led to competitive pressures on banks to take riskier investment decisions (Roach, 2009; Roubini & Mihm, 2011). Added to this, it has been indicated that long-term wage stagnation (principally in the United States) from the 1980s, coupled with low interest rates, meant that spending was maintained through personal indebtedness: much of this was instrumentalized through sub-prime mortgages to low income groups, partially or crudely sustainable when house prices were rising (thereby reducing the real value of the debt) but unsustainable otherwise, and with catastrophic consequences when prices declined (Crouch, 2008; Rajan, 2010). But perhaps the most significant aspects were in the policy assumptions and underlying thinking which believed in the ultimate self-correction of markets (via tendency of markets to reach equilibrium and the use of 'sound' fiscal and monetary policy to keep public debt and inflation in order) and the positive value of innovation in this important sector of the economy. Lost from this thinking was the view that deregulated self-interest in a market economy can lead to 'bubble, mania, panic and burst' (Akerlof & Shiller, 2009; De Grauwe, 2008). One may add that even the most cursory historical insight (e.g. railway building booms and busts in 19th century Britain and the United States, or further back the early 18th century South Sea Bubble) may have been useful had of course the lessons been learned: that speculation based on the belief of potentially large and increasing returns, but based on flimsy or unrealistic views of economic or market demand, can lead to asset and business crash. From the global financial crisis, the resulting fall in confidence in the banking system to extend credit and lend resulted in a sharp and severe recession, added to a piling of debt on public sector finances as governments had to bail out stressed banks.

Some leading commentators noted that 'the dominance of the neo-liberal, Washington consensus policies at the onset of the global financial crisis was not, in the view of many, mere co-incidence but rather the global financial crisis was a result of them – inadequate regulation fostered by the neo-liberal critique left financial institutions free to engage in risky practices – [and] the abolition of capital controls that now allowed the financial crisis to spread around the world' (Grant & Wilson, 2012, p. 6). One could therefore assume that such policy failure leading to near financial institutional collapse and resulting recession would lead to policy change. And indeed for a time, this appeared to be the case. The United States nationalized AIG, the colossal insurance company, and acquired General Motors; the Federal Reserve Board undertook a major programme of quantitative easing and bought vast quantities of toxic assets from the banks (Troubled Assets Relief Programme – TARP). The UK government recapitalized the wrecked Royal Bank of Scotland and helped recapitalize a newly merged HBOS-Lloyds TSB (at a cost over £40 billion) (*Economist*, 21 February 2009, p. 56). The UK government under Prime Minister Brown introduced a stimulus package, and in 2009 in President Obama's first term the American Recovery and Reinvestment Act was estimated to be worth $83 billion over a 10 year period including direct spending on infrastructure, education, health, energy, taxation incentives and social benefits. A respected *Financial Times* commentator wrote of the post-2008 environment thus:

> Politicians forced to support private banks with public money could no longer deny that government safety nets are a natural and necessary feature of social reality, whether in financial markets, or fire fighting – The upshot was that the market fundamentalist opposition between government and private enterprise could no longer be seriously maintained. (Kaletsky, 2010, p. 8)

The Response: Same Old – Same Old

Beyond the immediate and crisis-induced responses to the global financial crisis and its aftermath, there is mixed evidence on the extent to which there is an extant or developing model of state engagement to accept key roles and responsibilities which thereby challenge the neo-liberal NPM privileging of markets, deregulation (and in service provision) associated approaches to accountability. First there is only sporadic evidence that regulatory activity of the very financial products at the heart of the crisis ('over the counter' derivatives products like credit default swaps and collateralized debt obligations) is occurring. The profitability of the financial sector in the early years of the 21st century (especially 2002–2007) created a coalition of insiders with government comfort due to the subsequent tax take (Morgan, 2012). Detailed research has shown that such insiders still have an impact on policy: for example there has been no success at initial attempts to outlaw such trades, and subsequent attempts to place credit default swaps on regulated exchanges have been largely unsuccessful (Morgan, 2012), and although there has been some more success in pushing derivative-based products on to regulated exchanges in the United States (under the Dodd–Frank Act) (Morgan, 2012), there must remain some scepticism over the US system's willingness to go further – the financial sector supported Obama heavily in 2008, Goldman Sachs giving him three times the financial support it gave to his rival John McCain (opensecrets.org, cited in Wilson, 2012).

Second, in Europe the initial response to the crisis in 2008 saw the European Central Bank undertake positive measures to support liquidity and credit. Many continental countries (e.g. France and Germany) supported employment maintenance initiatives and some Nordic countries supported active social policies and labour market support measures (Hemerijck, 2013). But from 2010, after many countries were required to financially support their banks, running up deficits in the process, the European narrative altered to one of fiscal consolidation and austerity especially in the most indebted eurozone countries, where reductions in state entitlements and provision in pensions, public sector salaries, social benefits, retirement age etc were the policy prescriptions required for EU financial support. There seems little evidence of a new model developing despite some mixed signals from senior EU figures. For example:

> ... the [European] Commission does not believe that cutbacks are the solution to Europe's challenges ... sound public finances are an essential part of sustainable growth – to focus solely on cuts suggests that government over-spending was the only source of the crisis. In fact we all know that problems with the bahaviour and regulation of the financial sector, and problems of political will, are also factors in this crisis. (Barroso, 2011)

Third, in some leading European countries, left of centre parties (i.e. the parties one assumes would be more empathetic to an alternative to the neo-liberal approach) became locked in to the prevailing paradigm. For example, in the UK New Labour (and to a lesser extent the SPD in Germany and the Socialist Party in France) responded to the apparently politically successful low tax policies of their Conservative opponents by promising to match their spend policies (with no increases in income tax) if elected. And this they did when elected in 1997. Spending did increase at subsequent re-elections, but not as a result of new models of thinking, rather this was founded on a booming financial services sector, which subsequently ran into difficulty.

Fourth, the United States is in many ways intriguing. Critical tax and spend decisions are often gridlocked, at the current time caught between an executive willing to use public sector funding and activity for restructuring, reform and amelioration if not modification of neo-liberal approaches to economic management and a key part of the legislature (House of Representatives) antagonistic and hostile. Polling evidence and opinion survey consistently show Americans less enthusiastic about state involvement in economic matters. And the emergence of the Tea Party has forced the Republican Party to an anti-statist position in large measure. Yet at least one element of the neo-liberal model is roundly criticized: the over-privileging of big business especially banks. Yet this articulates itself as a fear that big government and big business were both complicit and indeed colluded in policies and practices that caused the financial crisis, and that the contrast in massive funding directed to bank rescue was in contrast to home-owner foreclosure (Wilson, 2012). This is quite consistent with a populist political tradition (Jacksonian democracy), which it is claimed has long-standing impact on US politics (Meyers, 1957), and of course does not sit easily with any notion that the state should be active in rebuilding a politico-economic model.

An Alternative Perspective: Adaptation and Resilience

There is however an alternative perspective. This suggests that the difficulty in identifying a new model of state engagement post-financial crash is not simply explained by the continuation of pre-existing neo-liberal approaches. Rather, that a number of countries have in fact actually adapted themselves to the neo-liberal, NPM environment is thereby obviating the appearance of an over-arching model.[1] These adaptive capacities, arguably system resilience, can be illustrated in a variety of settings. Most welfare state systems in western Europe and the EU since the 1980s have introduced measures to address economic and cost efficiencies usually aligned to labour market flexibility and deregulation. Social partners were involved in reforms in the Netherlands in the 1980s, then Denmark, Ireland and Finland; Italy, Portugal and Spain followed in the 1990s. Many traditional social security and insurance benefits (e.g. unemployment and sickness benefits) were altered and welfare to work schemes introduced and enhanced in scope (Huo, 2009). Some countries have introduced childcare support, altered parental leave arrangements largely motivated by the growing role of women in the workplace and the underlying facilitation for a flexible often feminized labour force – the dual-earner model. Scandinavian countries have often led the way here, but new EU members (Poland, Slovenia and Czech Republic) have been active in this direction (Hemerijck, 2013). The strong trend which has been identified has been categorized as a shift from social protection to the social promotion of economic and social policy (*ibid.*; Hay, 2004). Once again the United States presents an interesting case. Although state action is not part of the US tradition as it is in Europe, the economic crisis post-2008 led to rising numbers of unemployed workers with no proper access to health care – the hard fought reform over health care (though still to be implemented) can be considered as the state driving forward an adaptation to an important part of the security-welfare system, ameliorating some aspects and consequences of economic and market failure.

System adaptability or resilience has taken many forms. There is evidence that in some Scandinavian countries the quasi-corporatism exerted by social partners (peak labour and employer organizations) has displayed a degree of resilience against attempts at neo-liberal styled reforms. For instance the centralized wage bargaining in such systems has led to low-wage differentials between skill levels, so business has a motivation to eliminate low skilled jobs, and support high training and unemployment insurance; but it's only the employers organized collectively who will do this (very few will provide collective benefits on their own). This has led to high co-ordination of training and support for protection of core workers (Martin & Swank, 2012). In Denmark it has been said that 'business and labour are like Siamese twins' (cited in Martin, 2012) protecting their authority against the state (Martin & Swank, 2012). In Germany there is also a strong and well-structured peak level relationship between organized labour and business, underpinned by financial structures and high levels of human capital investment as well as support for competitive technological innovation. This has combined with a general reluctance by the state to directly intervene in social and economic matters, instead following the principles of 'ordo-liberalism' (Carlin, 1996) following rule-based policies to ensure competitiveness and lack of rent seeking by the powerful interest groups (*ibid.*; Crafts & Torlino, 2008). Germany has introduced adaptive social reforms in labour regulation, retirement policy, social insurance and flexible labour markets with childcare structures in support (Morel, Palier, & Palme, 2012). This has been done through social and political concentrtation (e.g. some policies proposed by social democrats, subsequently implemented by Christian democrats – Korthouwer, 2010) and broad support from the key social partners (unions and business) (Avdagic, Rhodes, & Visser, 2011).

There are two important nuances to the adaptivity argument. The first is the United Kingdom. The neo-liberal and NPM inspired drivers accentuating and privileging markets and other measures over state and bureaucratic organization and delivery certainly led to the strong UK adaptation, especially in the 1990s. New Labour's Third Way was positioned precisely thus: to stand as an alternative (a third way) to, on the one hand, state, and, on the other, private-market dominated thinking (Giddens, 1998). Modernization and reform of public services were justified thus (e.g. Le Grand, 2007). Outwith the UK, such thinking also gained some traction for a time among elected social democratic leaders in Europe – e.g Gerhard Schroder, Wim Kok, Poul Nyrup Rasmussen; some of these ideas also made their way into the European Commission (1999), and indeed the OECD (e.g. OECD, 1997). A detailed assessment of the third way and the extent to which it influenced policy is not the main purpose of this chapter, but what is clear is that the New Labour years did adapt traditional state and bureaucratic approaches (arguably continuing many adaptations undertaken in the 1980s). However, since 2010 the evidence is rather mixed. The political response of the UK Coalition Government which took power in 2010 has been radical rather than adaptive, that is premised on a more directly pro-market non-state focused approach: austerity driven, reducing public spending to reduce the public sector deficit and debt, and aiming to 're-balance the economy' from public to private, from finance to manufacturing (the latter has seemingly dropped off the political agenda) and in the management of many public services, shifting the delivery from the state towards individuals, communities and voluntary endeavour ('The Big Society') (Alderwick, 2012; HM Government, 2010). On the other hand, growing evidence does suggest significant elements of continuity with New Labour's approach. There is a notable gap between rhetoric and reality in regulatory reform, where a bonfire of quangos was promised to 'release business and civil society groups from the burden of regulation' (HM Government, 2010), but few quangos were abolished and those that were became absorbed into the core executive (Fitzpatrick & White, 2013); in public expenditure there are large cuts in local government spend, but cuts in welfare are actually curbing growth rather than major reductions, and health spending has been protected – though healthcare inflation and demographic change may mean real cuts in effect. Big Society thinking does not seem embedded in state policy: while there are a range of small and medium scale initiatives it is unlikely there will be a major devolution or transfer of budgets for delivery to local or societal groups, and indeed there is some scepticism of the capacity of such groups or bodies to deliver (Social Enterprise UK, 2012). Indeed some commentators suggest that the 2013 UK budget saw the government turn towards a distinctly Keynesian approach to stimulate growth in the house construction sector through a loan guarantee system (Hutton, *Observer*, 24 March 2013), though this seems unlikely.

The second nuance is a number of significant states in Europe bordering on dysfunctionality; here the evidence would suggest the adaptivity argument is difficult to apply. Greece and Italy provide illustration. The Greek state has in the recent past made attempts to adjust tax, spend and benefit programmes to bring the state within long-term sustainability norms, e.g. property taxes and pension reforms from 2008, but the failure to reform the administration of the state and the inability to collect tax (to date) seriously questions any viable model of state accountability and responsibility (Matsaganis, 2011) under present circumstances, especially if EU support terms severely limit growth prospects and economic performance. In Italy, an insider clientist labour market system has not been reformed despite periods of austerity. An austerity package in 2011 included almost €25 billion by the reduction in transfers to sub-national regions, increase in pension age, wage freeze in public sector etc. This led to a series of strikes, massive unpopularity in the government (under Berlusconi) and eventually the eurozone crisis resulting in loss of market confidence and the formation of a technocratic government under Mario Monti (Schmidt, 2012). At the time of writing (April 2013) it is unclear who will form the next government after no clear majority has been obtained in the 2013 election.

CONCLUSION

Finally, having traversed from a traditional bureaucratic state where accountability of services was through bureaucratic hierarchies to a market influenced neo-liberal NPM environment accountable to market and performance norms, there is (as a result of the discrediting of the neo-liberal approach), a 'paradigm gap': as yet, there is no recognized organizing framework with a 'new' politico-economic paradigm outlining the role and responsibility of the state. An explanation for this has been provided in the chapter. But in this gap or (perhaps) transitional space where does accountability and responsibility lie for provision of public services? What can be shown with some confidence is a diversity and patchwork of experience, leading some to believe that various approaches as they have evolved (e.g. traditional bureaucratic, to NPM, to approaches based on governance and partnerships – 'new public governance') have been layered and co-exist (Hartley, 2005). This can be seen vividly in the United Kingdom where there continues to be significant outsourcing and marketization in areas of labour market and welfare activity: job placement operates on a market and contract performance accountability basis; elements of healthcare provision may move this way too with NHS reform in England – the Health and Social Care Act has opened up competition to a diversity of providers (public, private and other) who can be funded to provide health care on behalf of public funded NHS patients. On the other hand there are examples of privatized, marketized or outsourced activities being returned to state control and therefore directly publically accountable. For example in the United Kingdom, East Coast line franchised private rail operator, National Express, withdrew from operating the line in 2009; the service was then directly run through a vehicle retained by UK government for such a backstop situation (in effect re-nationalized), since when it has been running as one of the United Kingdom's most successful operation, making returns to the UK Treasury, reinvesting in rolling stock and scoring highly on customer satisfaction; UK government intend to return this line to a private operator via a franchise by 2015. Also in the United Kingdom, the devolved Welsh government initially created an arms length body for the funding of post-16 education establishments in Wales, using a performance agreement to monitor performance; it was subsequently wound up and brought into the Welsh government core executive. Sweden, in the early mid-2000s privatized much of its welfare state in particular pensions, childcare and a range of labour market policy areas; however after the 2008 financial crisis it centralized back to state provision (Niklausson, 2011). And recently in the United Kingdom (March 2013), an arms length agency the UK Borders Agency was abolished, its functions split and returned to the core executive (the UK Home Office).

In fact what could be said is that the future of public services and how accountability is organized is at a crossroads. As two leading academics said in evidence to a House of Commons Committee about public service activity: *it could be delivered as locally as possible, and preferably by independent individuals or private or voluntary groups, unless the tasks were beyond their capacity; it would be organized and delivered with the least possible formal intervention by the state; it would involve as much public participation as possible; it would simply be abandoned by public authorities without alternative arrangements being made* (Hood & Lodge, 2011, p. 56). Each of these scenarios of course have different accountability arrangements, ranging from direct participation and a form of participative accountability to local or community accountability, market or organizational performance accountability, or complete state withdrawal and so no accountability at all.

For the future this leads to two possible developments. First, that public services will be increasingly provided in a variety of ways, a patchwork and diversity of provision, using various modes and instruments of accountability and with continued definition and re-definition of what should be directly accountable to government. Second, that there will be politically articulated policies with a cohering narrative (like the Keynesian 'post-war settlement', or NPM-Neo Liberalism) about the role of government and public sector organizations in service provision. In the current post-financial crisis austerity era, this latter development does not as yet appear to be occurring.

NOTE

1. There is an alternative view which downplays 'adaptivity'. For example, it is suggested that over the medium to long term (say the 1980s and 1990s) the political attack on social spending, trade union power along with deregulation and privatization weakened traditional working class politics. Concomitantly, prosperity led to blurring of class boundaries and electoral confusion enabling successive governments to abandon post-war consensus politics, shifting income from labour to capital. The adverse consequences of the deregulated capital and market favouring approach to policy have been displayed by the global financial crisis, yet no new paradigm or consensus on such has emerged because new political thinking, politicians experimenting with new approaches to problems has barely begun (Hall, 2013).

REFERENCES

Akerlof, G. A., & Shiller, R. J. (2009). *Animal spirits: How human psychology drives the economy and why it matters for global capitalism*. Princeton NJ: Princeton University Press.

Alderwick, H. (2012). Continuity with new labour? Deconstructing the triangulation of David Cameron's conservatives. *Journal of Politics and International Studies*, *7*(Summer), 1–49.

Avdagic, S., Rhodes, M., & Visser, J. (2011). *Social pacts in Europe: Emergence, evolution and institutionalization*. Oxford: Oxford University Press.

Barroso. (2011). State of the Union Address. Retrieved from http://www.ec.europa.eu/avservices/services/showshortlist.do?film

Baumgartner, F., & Jones, B. (1993). *Agendas and instability in American politics*. Chicago IL: Chicago University Press.

Beland, D., & Cox, R. H. (2013). Politics of policy paradigms. *Governance*, *26*(2), 193–195.

Burnham, J., & Horton, S. (2013). *Public management in the United Kingdom. A new introduction*. Basingstoke: Palgrave Macmillan.

Carlin, W. (1996). West German growth and institutions 1945-90, In N. Crafts and G. Torlino (Eds.) *Economic growth in Europe since 1945*. Cambridge: Cambridge University Press.

Crafts, N., & Torlino, G. (2008) *European economic growth 1950–2005: An overview*. Centre for Economic Policy Research Paper No. 6863.
Crouch, C. (2008). What will follow the demise of privatized Keynesianism? *The Political Quarterly*, *79*(4), 476–487.
Crouch, C. (2011). *The strange non-death of neo-liberalism*. Cambridge: Polity.
De Grauwe, P. (2008). Animal spirits and monetary policy. *Economic Theory*, *47*(2), 453–458.
Economist. (2009), *Thanks Gordon. Why bankers should beware prime ministers promoting mergers*. 21 February.
European Commission. (1999). *Employment in Europe*. Luxembourg: Office for the Official Publications of the European Communities.
Fenwick, J., Johnston Miller, K., & McTavish, D. (2012). Co-governance or meta-bureaucracy? Perspectives of local governance 'partnership'. *Policy and Politics*, *40*(3), 405–422.
Fitzpatrick, D., & White, A. (2013). The crisis of regulation. In D. Richards, M. J. Smith & C. Hay (Eds.), *Institutional crisis in twenty first century Britain*. Basingstoke: Palgrave Macmillan.
Giddens, A. (1998). *The third way: The renewal of social democracy*. Cambridge: Polity.
Grant, W. and Wilson, G. K. (Eds.) (2012). Introduction, In *The consequences of the global financial crisis*. Oxford: Oxford University Press
Hall, D. (2005). *Evaluating the impact of liberalization on public services*. Report commissioned by European Federation of Public Service Unions. Retrieved from http://www/psriu.org/reports/2008
Hall, P. A. (2013). Brother can you paradigm? *Governance*, *26*(2), 189–192.
Hartley, J. (2005). Innovations in governance and public services: Past and present. *Public Money and Management*, *25*(1), 27–34.
Hay, C. (2004). Common trajectories, variable paces, divergent outcomes? Models of European capitalism under conditions of complex economic interdependence. *Review of International Political Economy*, *11*(2), 231–262.
Hayek, F. A. (1944). *The road to serfdom*. London: Routledge and Kegan Paul.
Heclo, H. (1978). Issue networks and the executive establishment. In A. King (Ed.), *The new American political system*. Washington, DC: American Enterprise Institute.
Hemerijck, A. (2013). *Changing welfare states*. Oxford: Oxford University Press.
HM Government. (2010). *The coalition: Our programme for government*. London: TSO.
Hood, C., & Lodge, M. (2011). *The post bureaucratic age. Some analytic challenges, change in government. The agenda for leadership*. Public Administration Select Committee HC 714, 56–58. London: TSO.
Hughes, O. (2012). *Public management and administration. An introduction*. Basingstoke. Palgrave Macmillan.
Huo, J. (2009). *Third way reforms: Social democracy after the golden age*. Cambridge: Cambridge University Press.
Hutton, Will (2013). *The Chancellor is for turning after all. And whisper it, he's switching to Keynes*. 24 March.
Jordan, A. G., & Maloney, W. A. (1997). Accounting for sub governments: Explaining the persistence of policy communities. *Administration and Society*, *29*(5), 557–583.
Jordan, G. (1981). Iron triangles, wooly corporatism and elastic nets: Images of the policy process. *Journal of Public Policy*, *1*(1), 95–123.
Kaletsky, A. (2010). *Capitalism 4.0: The birth of a new economy*. London: Bloomsbury.
Kickert, W. (1997). Public governance in the Netherlands: An alternative to Anglo-American 'managerialism'. *Public Administration*, *75*, 731–752.

Kickert, W. (2003). Beneath consensual corporatism: Traditions of governance in the Netherlands. *Public Administration*, *81*, 119–140.

Klein, R. (1995). *The new politics of the NHS*. London: Longman.

Korthouwer, G. H. P. (2010). *Party politics as we knew it? Failure to dominate government, intra-party dynamics and welfare reforms in continental Europe*. Oisterwijk: Uitgeuerij Box Press.

Kreiger, J. (1986). *Reagan, Thatcher and the politics of decline*. Cambridge: Polity Press.

Le Grand, J. (2007). The politics of choice and competition in public services. *Political Quarterly*, *78*(2), 207–213.

Martin, C. J. (2012). Social solidarity in Scandinavia after the fall of finance capitalism. In W. Grant & G. K. Wilson (Eds.), *The consequences of the global financial crisis*. Oxford: Oxford University Press.

Martin, C. J., & Swank, D. (2012). *The political construction of business interests: Co-ordination, growth and equality*. New York, NY: Cambridge University Press.

Massey, A., & Pyper, R. (2005). *Public management and modernization in Britain*. Basingstoke: Palgrave Macmillan.

Matsaganis, M. (2011). The welfare state and the crisis: The case of Greece. *Journal of European Social Policy*, *21*, 501–512.

Meyers, M. (1957). *The Jacksonian persuasion: Politics and beliefs*. Stanford: Stanford University Press.

Morel, N., Palier, B., & Palme, J. (2012). *Towards a social investment welfare state? Ideas, policies, challenges*. Bristol: Policy.

Morgan, G. (2012). Constructing financial markets: Reforming over-the-counter derivatives markets in the aftermath of the financial crisis. In W. Grant & G. Wilson (Eds.), *The consequences of the global financial crisis. The rhetoric of reform and regulation*. Oxford: Oxford University Press.

Niklausson, L. (2011). *Forming a regional policy in Sweden: Where will the contradictory policies lead?* Unpublished manuscript, cited in Martin, C. J. (2012). Social solidarity in Scandinavia after the fall of finance capitalism. In W. Grant & G. K. Wilson (2012) (Eds.) *The consequences of the global financial crisis*. Oxford: Oxford University Press.

Niskanen, W. A. (1971). *Bureaucracy and representative government*. Chicago, IL: Adline.

Niskanen, W. A. (1973). *Bureaucracy, servant or master? Lessons from America*. London: Institute of Economic Affairs.

Niskanen, W. A. (1994). *Bureaucracy and public economics*. Cheltenham: Edward Elgar.

OECD. (1997). *Beyond 2000: The new social policy agenda*. OECD Working Papers v (43), Paris.

OECD. (2005). *Modernising government. The way forward*. Paris: OECD.

OECD. (2008). *The state of the public service*. Paris: OECD.

Osborne, D., & Gaebler, T. (1992). *Re-inventing government: How the entrepreneurial spirit is transforming the public sector*. Reading MA: Addison-Wesley.

Osborne, S. P. (2006). The new public governance. *Public Management Review*, *8*(3), 377–387.

Peters, J. (2012). Neo-liberal convergence in North America and Western Europe: Fiscal austerity, privatization and public sector reforms. *Review of International Political Economy*, *19*(2), 208–235.

Pollitt, C. (2007). Convergence or divergence. What has been happening in Europe'. In C. Pollitt, S. van Thiel & V. Homburg (Eds.), *New public management in Europe: Adaptation and alternatives*. Basingstoke: Macmillan.

Pollitt, C., & Bouckaert, G. (2004). *Public management reform. A comparative analysis*. Oxford: Oxford University Press.
Pollock, A., Leys, C., & Price, D. (2005). *NHS plc: The privatization of our health care*. New York, NY: Verso.
Posner, R. A. (2009). *A failure of capitalism: The case of '08 and the decent into depression*. Cambridge MA: Harvard University Press.
Rajan, R. (2010). *Fault lines: How hidden fractures still threaten the world economy*. Princeton, NJ: Princeton University Press.
Reich, R. (2008). *Supercapitalism: The battle for democracy in an age of big business*. Cambridge: Icon Books.
Roach, S. (2009). Leadership imperatives for a post-crisis world. In A. Hemerijck, B. Knapen & E. van Doorne (Eds.), *Aftershocks: Economic crisis and institutional choice*. Amsterdam: Amsterdam University Press.
Roubini, N., & Mihm. (2011). *Crisis economics*. London: Penguin.
Schmidt, V. A. (2012). What happened to the state influenced market economies (SMEs)? France, Italy and Spain confront the crisis as the good, the bad, and the ugly. In W. Grant & G. K. Wilson (Eds.), *The consequences of the global financial crisis*. Oxford: Oxford University Press.
Skidelsky, R. (2009). *Keynes: The return of the master*. London: Allen Lane.
Social Enterprise UK. (2012). *The shadow state: A report about the outsourcing of services*. London: Social Enterprise UK.
Tett, G. (2010). *Fool's gold*. London: Abacus.
Van Dooren, W., Bouckaert, G., & Halligan, J. (2010). *Performance management in the public sector*. Abingdon: Routledge.
Weir, M. (1989). The spread of Keynesianism in the United States. In P. A. Hall (Ed.), *The political power of economic ideas*. Princeton, NJ: Princeton University Press.
Wilson, G. (2012). The United States: The strange survival of (neo)liberalism. In W. Grant & G. K. Wilson (Eds.), *The consequences of the global financial crisis*. Oxford: Oxford University Press.

LOCAL GOVERNMENT IN ENGLAND: FAULT LINES IN ETHICAL GOVERNANCE?

Michael Macaulay, Gary Hickey and Norjahan Begum

ABSTRACT

Purpose – *This chapter looks at the development of the concepts of ethical governance within the English local government structure. It examines this development by reference both to the current crisis in funding and service provision, and also to the development of standards for good governance and integrity.*

Design – *The chapter draws upon a national survey that was conducted by the authors in 2012.*

Findings – *The chapter suggests that while there may have been a wish to create more opportunities for devolved decision-making in English local government through changes in legislation, those policy-makers surveyed thought that the structures and processes of decision-making might be weakened.*

Looking for Consensus?: Civil Society, Social Movements and Crises for Public Management
Critical Perspectives on International Public Sector Management, Volume 2, 25–44

ISSN: 2045-7944/doi:10.1108/S2045-7944(2013)0000002003

Implications – *The chapter indicates not just the need for further studies but also a more holistic exploration of the relationships between the ideas of 'good governance' and whose different interests are met through such changes.*

Keywords: Accountability; ethics; integrity; governance

INTRODUCTION

The *Localism Act 2011* wrought a significant number of changes to the landscape of local government in England, which will doubtless keep academics occupied for many years to come. One area that has received comparatively less attention than others is the creation of a new integrity framework (in part 1, chapter 7 of the Act), which came into force in July 2012. The framework replaces the old regime that was established by the *Local Government Act 2000* and sees a considerable reduction in the scale, scope and sanctions for issues pertaining to standards of conduct. Even more recently, the *Local Audit and Accountability Bill* was unveiled during the 2013 Queen's Speech. Again under the banner of localism, the Bill formally abolishes the Audit Commission although this had long been anticipated. Perhaps more important, and certainly more far-reaching, is what will be the new form of public audit, which leads to numerous questions of quite serious potential conflicts of interest. In short, the nature of integrity and accountability is currently being transformed in English local government.

The UK legislation fits neatly into a burgeoning research interest in local integrity and governance, which is particularly prevalent in Australia and Continental Europe (see, e.g., Head, Brown, & Connors, 2008; Huberts, Anechiarico, & Six, 2008; Salminen, Ikola-Norrbacka, & Rinna, 2009). Along with other key public values accountability and transparency, integrity continues to be viewed as a key component in public governance. Integrity has been positively linked with efficiency (de Graaf and van der Wal, 2010); effectiveness (Matei, Matei, & Savulescu, 2010); and public trust both in the United Kingdom and in Europe (Cowell, Downe, & Morgan, 2011). Perhaps most importantly, public sector organisations with either low or high integrity have been found to impact on the ethical culture (Jennings, 2006) and the quality of leadership of that organisation (Lawton & Macaulay, 2009; Macaulay, Hickey, & Begum, 2011; Trevino, Brown, & Hartman, 2003).

Recent research has increasingly looked at the ways in which integrity management relates to overall governance (Head, 2012), which has led one commentator to suggest that the development of local integrity shifts the debate from good governance to 'good enough' governance (Evans, 2012). NGOs are also getting involved in local integrity; in July 2013, for example, Transparency International launched a pilot study for its new Local Integrity System (LIS) model, closely modelled on its well-established National Integrity System (NIS) approach.

This chapter will, therefore, map these changes and discuss the implications for the future of English local government. In particular it will draw on a national survey conducted by the authors in June 2012, which evaluated the perceptions of local government officers in relation to what was then the impending arrival of the new integrity framework (Macaulay et al., 2012). The officers expressed serious concerns that such changes potentially weaken the governance structures of local government, and that the new regime would neither enhance local integrity nor create local trust. Thus we will suggest that ethical fault lines have been unearthed by the *Localism Act 2011*, and that these have been potentially deepened by the impending changes detailed in the *Local Audit and Accountability Bill*. We will then suggest that 'good enough' governance is not, in this case, good enough at all and that a more systematic approach is required. In order to begin this conversation, however, it may be useful to have a brief exploration of the development of academic interest in local integrity.

Local Integrity Systems

The Local Integrity System (LIS) concept came to recent prominence fairly recently with the publication of two important works: Huberts et al.'s (2008) *Local Integrity Systems* and Head et al.'s (2008) *Promoting Integrity*. Each provide a fascinating picture of the way in which different local areas have established and developed responses to corruption and issues of difficult governance. Huberts et al. (2008) offer examples from (among others) Amsterdam, Sydney, London, Antwerp and Hamburg. Head et al. (2008) provides LIS responses from, among others, the Pacific islands, New South Wales, and the Australian Wheat Board. Each book aims to provide a framework for suitable comparative research: 'the comparative perspective can show us how robust and valid our theoretical and policy presuppositions actually are' (Huberts et al., 2008, p. 5), and each acknowledges a debt to the National Integrity System (NIS) concept originally developed by Transparency International.

The NIS is characterised as a Greek temple, upon which 13 institutional pillars (e.g. legislature, executive, anti-corruption agencies, civil society) stand on the political, economic, legal and social foundations. Some see the metaphor as inappropriate, and the NIS has recently been described as birds' nest rather than a Greek temple, i.e. an amalgamation of fairly weak institutional arrangements that still manage to provide stability and strength in public integrity (Sampford, Smith, & Brown, 2005). Notwithstanding the appropriateness of different metaphors, there are at least two important concerns regarding the NIS model. The first of these concerns is the extent to which the NIS model provides reasonable comparisons. Transparency International has conducted over 80 NIS country reports, yet has admitted that they do not provide a particularly sound basis for comparison, so much so that it has substantially altered its methodology (see, e.g., the recent UK study published in 2011) to include a more quantitative component. Nevertheless Transparency International still suggests that the NIS results are not directly comparable with each other:

> since there is no international board which reviews and calibrates all scores to ensure that the same information, methodology, and judgment process have been used across countries, we do not produce any country rankings and do not recommend using the raw scores for cross-country comparisons. (TI, 2012)

The difficulty with the LIS concept is that comparisons may become even more difficult to sustain: one may reasonably ask, for example, how the experiences of the Australian Wheat Board truly chime with the experiences of the Hong Kong Anti-Corruption Commission, or the standards committee for the Greater London Authority. It is crucial for comparative research that there are key touchstones, which allow for generalisability and validity in findings and using a simple case study approach may not yet offer such a platform for analytical synthesis.

The second concern, and possibly a more substantial one, is the extent to which NIS or LIS concepts actually show a *system*. Pope (2009, p. 24), who was the progenitor of the NIS concept for Transparency International, was clear that the NIS should be the product of rational and deliberate design: 'such accountability measures, when designed as part of a national effort to reduce corruption, comprise an integrity "system"'. By this logic, any measures that may have been developed on an ad hoc basis cannot, therefore, constitute a NIS. Head et al. (2009, p. 5) disagree: the design element of an integrity system is a conditional factor: 'every society already has some kind of "integrity system," even if not widely understood, or recognised, or respected for its achievements. If there were no elements of an integrity system in place, then social and political order itself would collapse'. Lawton and Six (2010) suggested something in between, that an integrity system could be understood in terms of fuzzy sets, membership of which can allow a more fluid movement within a complex system. Similarly, Maesschalck and Bertok (2009) identify four functions of an integrity management system: defining integrity, guiding towards integrity, monitoring integrity and enforcing integrity. Such approaches go beyond the institutional analysis, therefore, to look at relationships between organisation, role and function.

These differing perspectives pose a crucial question: if an integrity system is uncodified to the extent that many people would not even recognise it as such, then can it be considered as a system at all? It may be argued, of course, that the initial NIS model is no more than a useful metaphor, and therefore it does not really matter what type of system (if any) it is. Yet this is not the view held by the majority of its supporters, and therefore it remains an important question. The newly proposed LIS methodology by Transparency International has taken this view into account, as well as looking at the institutional pillars (as it does for the NIS) it also necessitates an anlaysis of local power to reveal how relationships between institutions work and where these may need to be moved in the future. Without such underpinnings, the system aspect of the LIS becomes somewhat redundant, and again the comparative aspect is reduced to simply looking at individual case studies in order to ascertain what (if anything) fits together.

We will now have a look at the local government integrity framework that was established in the *Local Government Act 2000*. We will argue that it certainly constituted a system as understood by Lawton and Six, or Maesschalck and Bertok but that more importantly, it was a system that was recognised, well understood and generally well supported by local government members and officers alike.

English Local Government and the Integrity Management System

The framework that was established in the *Local Government Act 2000* was very much a child of its time and arose as a direct response to a number of high-profile fraud and corruption scandals in English local government. The framework covered 8,787 local authorities (351 principal councils and

8,350 Parish and Town councils) and built upon a number of recommendations from the third report of the Committee on Standards in Public Life (1997). The English integrity framework was born out of a perceived crisis in local government following several high profile scandals, including major fraud and corruption cases in Westminster, Hull and perhaps most notably Doncaster Metropolitan Council. This latter case became known as "Donnygate" and resulted in 35 convictions of local politicians and council officers. As a result New Labour commissioned the Committee on Standards in Public Life to hold an enquiry, which found that contrary to external perception, ethical standards in local government were really quite high and that, if anything, the sector was already extremely tightly regulated, being held accountable to a number of external agencies (Local Government Ombudsman, Audit Commission, District Audit) as well as the then Office for the Deputy Prime Minister (now Department for Communities and Local Government).

As a result the CSPL report made it clear that responsibility for local standards must remain local: 'the basis for any system of good governance must be for the primary responsibility to be given to those in charge of the organisation itself' (CSPL, 1997, p. 43). The resulting framework therefore comprised a number of key pillars: (1) a mandatory code of conduct; (2) local standards committees to be established in every council; (3) new registers of interest; and (4) the creation of a national regulatory body, *Standards Board for England.* This latter element was the only major point of departure from the CSPL's recommendations, which created a series of problems that remained until SBE's abolition by the *Localism Act 2011.*

First, there was an initial suspicion that the Standards Board was a politically motivated creation, which was even questioned – and rejected – by the then Labour government itself:

> Maintaining an arms-length relationship with both central and local government is important to reinforce the message to the public that the Board will deal with any complaints in a rigorous yet impartial manner. (ODPM, 2005, p. 7)

The second, and perhaps more pertinent, issue was concern that the standards framework was simply too expensive, especially as the number of cases across England was relatively low. Macaulay, Newman, Lucas, and Peake (2010) demonstrated that, taking into account the Parish and Town councils, there was an average of 0.3% complaints per local authority in 2008/09. Furthermore out of the 733 cases referred for investigation in 2008/09, only 233 were actually subject to a full investigation and Table 1 shows the types of sanctions used to enforce these breaches, as well as the very low

Table 1. Number and Type of Sanctions Used in Dealing with Local Standards of Conduct.

Sanction	2008–09	2009–10
Censure	86	23
Apology	75	19
Training	83	10
Suspend	77	8
Refer to APE	10	0
Conciliation	3	0
Partly suspend	6	3
Restrict Access	1	0

number of sanctions used (NB more than one sanction can apply to an individual case).

Despite such criticisms, at one time the English local integrity framework was seen as a leader in its field, so much so that in a review of its earlier report, the Committee for Standards in Public Life (2005) described it as follows:

> The ethical standards framework for local government, as set out in Part III of the Local Government Act 2000, is arguably the most extensive and comprehensive statutory framework for standards of conduct of any group of public office-holders in the UK.

Certainly one can see how it worked in accordance with the basic principles of the integrity management model. The defining function of the framework was done by the code of conduct, which established the values of the integrity framework and also translated these into rules to make then practically understood. The leading function was conducted a range of stakeholders: principally local standards committees but also the local Monitoring Officer, political leaders and even the Chief Executive of the authority (Lawton, Iles, Llewellyn, Macaulay, & Thompson, 2005). Monitoring was undertaken, again, by the standards committee working in conjunction with the Monitoring Officer and was done, for example, through adherence to the registers of interest. Finally enforcement was conducted through the sanctions outlined above.

Early criticisms, however, hinted at a deeper and more fundamental issue in the standards framework: the relationship between central and local government. This became manifested in a crisis of *trust* that was highlighted in the second CSPL local government enquiry in 2005. The 1997 report argued that there was 'a suspicious attitude on the part of central government towards local government' (CSPL, 1997, p. 40) that was manifested in the creation of the Standards Board itself: central government considered an independent agency to be the most effective way to dispel public concern that corruption within local authorities was endemic, especially after such high profile-scandals as Doncaster. Moreover there was concern that dealing with ethics and standards at the local level may form an impression that local authorities were simply looking after their own. Such a view was still existent in recent comparative research of England, Scotland and Wales in which stakeholders expressed concern that the English framework had not been designed according to any particular principles:

> The framework that has emerged has been largely a political solution rather than the rational solutions that have emerged in the Scottish system and the Welsh system. (Macaulay, Hickey, & Newman, 2010)

The CSPL's (2005) review again highlighted the divisions between central and local. It argued that attempts to increase localisation had not gone far enough and recommended changes to the legislation to facilitate the CSPL's original vision of local authorities dealing with local issues. Despite initial resistance from central government, whose own ODPM review of 2005 argued that centralisation was a strength rather than a weakness, there was eventually an acceptance that localisation was the way forward in terms of investigations. Thus the *Local Government and Public Health Act* 2007 allowed local standards committees much more flexibility in investigating local complaints, and also bolstered their independence through legislating for the requirement to have an independent (i.e. a co-opted member) as the Chair. Meanwhile the Standards Board for England, rebranded *SfE*, became 'a strategic arms-length body dealing only with the most serious cases nationally and ensuring capacity is increased at local level through increased support, advice and guidance' (DCLG, 2005, p. 10).

In the run up to the 2010 general election in the United Kingdom, the Conservative Party pledged to reform local government in a number of ways. One of the most vague, but certainly very serious, pledges was to abolish the 'standards board regime'. Once the coalition government had been formed this pledge became enshrined in the *Localism Bill* but it was no less puzzling as there was little, if any, indication of what the 'standards board regime' meant.

There is little doubt that of all the elements of the standards framework, the Standards Board for England had borne the brunt of public and media criticism. Nevertheless the other elements of the framework had been shown repeatedly to be both valued and valuable. Macaulay et al. (2010) demonstrated that in general this move towards the local was welcomed by stakeholders across the framework. The majority of respondents in that study were convinced that the English framework should remain a local system:

> I would caution against more centralisation, not least because that's a huge role and these things can be dealt with quite quickly.

Reactions to the Localism Act 2011 *and the New Integrity Framework*

The *Localism Act 2011* has transformed the integrity framework of English local government. It has, perhaps unsurprisingly, abolished the Standards Board for England but has far more surprisingly abolished local standards committees as well. In their place the Act has placed a statutory duty to appoint an 'independent person' to oversee local authority decisions, and also a new law of failing to declare a pecuniary interest. It has, at the behest of the House of Lords, retained a revised code of conduct. Each of these brings substantial challenges.

Similarly, numerous studies demonstrated that the code enjoyed broad support (Committee for Standards in Public Life, 2005; Lawton and Macaulay, 2005, 2006; Office of the Deputy Prime Minister, 2005). The most recent research (Macaulay et al., 2010) suggests that the code remains highly valued and it was the one element that was robustly defended in the House of Lords, whereas the authors' survey found that a majority of respondents (57%) disagreed that a new code of conduct was necessary (Macaulay et al., 2012).

Section 28 (1) of the *Localism Act* simply states that the Code must enshrine the seven principles of public life (established in 1995 by the CSPL): selflessness, integrity, objectivity, accountability, openness, honesty, and leadership. Apart from that, however, the code is left on to the local authority's interpretation, which clearly plays along into the hands of localism. However, it also brings with it an attendant set of challenges. First, the form and clauses of a code of conduct can take substantial amounts of time to develop, and it is entirely probable that most local authorities will (in the short term at least) simply stick to the code they currently have. Second, it places immense pressure on the local Monitoring Officer to keep the code updated. Previous research has shown that the Monitoring Officer is the person most likely to bear the brunt of changes to the standards framework (Lawton et al., 2005) and with the removal of other major bodies any support networks no longer exist. Finally, perhaps the single biggest challenge is that of interpreting and translating the values of public life. How, for example, is one to judge a failure of leadership, or a failure of selflessness?

Initial plans in the *Localism Bill* was to abolish the statutory code of conduct altogether, a move rejected by the House of Lords (Hansard, 30 October, 2010). Instead the *Localism Act* chapter 7, 27(2) states that all local authorities have a duty to promote high standards of conduct through the implementation of a code of conduct. Section 28, however, makes it clear that the code must be founded on the seven principles of public life (selflessness, integrity, objectivity, accountability, openness, honesty and leadership) and that it must include a register of '(a) pecuniary interests, and (b) interests other than pecuniary interests' (section 28 (2)). Other than these provisions there is no guidance on what should or should not be in the code of conduct. This led to Lord Tope to declare:

> I am probably one of the greatest localists in your Lordships' House, but I thought at the time, and feel very strongly now, that if there is one thing that should not be left to local, it is standards in public life. We have got to the point that we have now reached because in the past there has been rather too much discretion over standards in public life. I am very pleased that we are going to have a mandatory code – or, rather, that it is going to be mandatory to have a code – but I am a little sad that its minimum provisions are not to be the same throughout the country.

Monitoring Officer's reactions to the changes in the code were similarly muted: just over one-third (36%) believed that any form of change was needed (Macaulay et al., 2012), and the majority of local authorities intended to simply adopt their existing code or a new model code of conduct devised by the *Local Government Association* (http://www.local.gov.uk/c/document_library/get_file?uuid=4735b8b0-5646-4abb-bc2e-23428614c621&groupId=10171, accessed 6 May 2013).

Moreover any breach of the code cannot be judged against legality or even ethics of outcomes, as the Section 28 (4) states:

> A failure to comply with a relevant authority's code of conduct is not to be dealt with otherwise than in accordance with arrangements made under subsection (6); in particular, a decision is not invalidated just because something that occurred in the process of making the decision involved a failure to comply with the code.

This appears to be an unusual piece of legislation. Decisions taken by councillors in breach of the code (e.g. decisions taken dishonestly or without regard to transparency) will remain valid, which appears paradoxical. As the Code is a statutory requirement, breaches of the code would normally be thought to be considered breaking the law. Yet in this case decisions being taken while in breach are not to be considered illegal.

The overarching value enshrined in the Act, hence its title, is the empowerment of local citizens and local authorities to make their own decisions. This value seems to have driven the changes to the code of conduct, which is far less prescriptive than the previous model version. The new statutory duty is to declare an interest (under Section 34) but this presents an interesting question. One of the criticisms levelled against the previous framework was that the public adopted a 'there's no smoke without fire' approach to investigations, so that even if found innocent of a breach of the code any councillor is likely to have her or his reputation tarnished. It remains to be seen what will happen to reputations once police investigations become the standard route for investigating councillors.

Another curious addition is the fate of standards committees. To all intents and purposes they have been abolished but there has been nothing to expressly state this and presumably (as was the case pre-2000) some authorities may yet choose to keep a form of committee, albeit one without any statutory function or authority. It seems ironic, therefore, that the changes brought by the coalition government have occurred under the very banner of the *Localism Act*. Nowhere is this more prevalent than in local standards committees. Although statutorily established in the *Local Government Act 2000*, 40% local authorities had already established a standards committee by 1999 (Doig & Skelcher, 2001, p. 3) and the *Local Government and Public Involvement in Health Act 2007* placed a statutory duty in having at least three independent members of the public sat on the committee (as well as the previously mentioned independent chair).

In early days, some local authorities had difficulty in finding and appointing independent members: research indicated that many independent members, although displaying a keen sense of civic duty, may not see their role as champions of an ethical organisation (Lawton et al., 2005, p. 103). Following the *2007 Act*, however, there was a much higher take-up of independent members and some authorities were noted for their recruitment practices (Lawton & Macaulay, 2009). Subsequent research (Lawton & Macaulay, 2009) showed that local standards committees were leading the way in developing notable practice in a number of areas in local governance (see Table 2).

Under the *Localism Act* there are no provisions for standards committees. Instead, Section 28 (7) mandates that

Table 2. Examples of Notable Practice in Local Standards Committees (Lawton & Macaulay, 2009).

Notable Practice	Case study authority
Organisational learning	Bristol City Council
Working with town and Parish councils	Taunton Deane Borough Council
Member development	Surrey Police Authority
Working with partnerships	Newark and Sherwood District Council
Recruitment and retention	South Cambridgeshire District Council
Training and development	Herefordshire County Council
Joint standards and audit committees	Runnymede Borough Council
High pressure investigations	Greater London Authority
Embedding standards	Newcastle City Council

> a relevant authority must include provision for the appointment by the authority of at least one independent person – (a) whose views are to be sought, and taken into account, by the authority before it makes its decision on an allegation that it has decided to investigate …

Section 28 (8) then states that the independent person cannot be appointed if she or he is a co-opted member of the authority, that is if she or he is a member of the existent standards committee, although as these committees were abolished as of 2012, there will be no co-opted members left. Again this has been met with concerns from Monitoring Officers: 79% felt that the standards committee was a crucial part of the integrity framework and 67% suggested that the committee would be retained within the authority in some form (albeit without any statutory functions).

What the *2011 Act* does require, however, is that each local authority must appoint at least one independent person (i.e. member of the public) to act as an ethical overseer for the council. Section 28 7 (a) states that

> the independent person's views are to be sought, and taken into account, by the authority before it makes its decision on an allegation that it has decided to investigate.

This person may be consulted by a member, co-opted member or Parish councillor (section 28 7 (b i, ii, iii)). While this clause still, clearly, gives some concession to the notion of independence, and by extension empowerment of the public to influence local authority decisions, the role and scope of independent members is greatly reduced. Moreover, as with the code of conduct, this part of the *2011 Act* is couched in extremely vague language. There is no formal arrangement for the seeking of view, nor an explanation as to what qualifies as views 'being taken into account', which may well mean that any independent views can be regularly ignored as long as some form of consultation has taken place.

Of course there is no indication as to how this person will be appointed either, although it is again likely that a member from existing standards committees will continue in some capacity, although the legislation remains unclear. Section 28 (8) (a) states that the independent member must not be a member, co-opted member or officer of the local authority. Independent members of standards committees would come under the category of co-opted members and would therefore appear to be ineligible from the role. While this may protect objectivity it would certainly lose a great deal of experience. It may even be the case that one person could act (semi)professionally as the independent advisor to a number of local authorities, although this may well lead to conflicts of interest. What can definitely lead to a conflict of interest is that the independent advisor is to be available to advise members under investigation and the officers in charge of the investigation, under Section 28 (7) (b). What the *Localism Act 2011* removes is certainly not being replaced with like-for-like.

Again these changes have met with considerable concern. Our national survey showed that 63% respondents agreed or strongly agreed that their local standards committee performed important non-statutory roles and that 79% respondents disagreed or strongly disagreed that the local standards committee was not needed.

Furthermore standards committees were seen as so important that just over two-thirds (67%) of respondents suggested that their local standards committee would not be disbanded. It remains to be seen in what form the non-statutory committees will exist, or indeed what their functions will be. In addition there were significant concerns attached to the newly developed role of the Independent Person: 68% respondents agreed or strongly agreed that the roles and responsibilities of the independent person had not been adequately explained in the legislation and as of June 2012, 90% respondents had neither identified nor appointed an independent person.

As with other aspects of the framework, therefore, there appears to be a need for greater clarity about the roles that the independent person will take. The roles as outlined in the legislation are so broad that many authorities are considering recruiting multiple independent persons or pooling with others.

This perhaps accounts for the number of standards committees that are being retained, despite the lack of statutory obligation to do so. As standards committees performed such a broad range of roles, it is interesting to note that they are being continued, which will, hopefully, help foster organisational learning and retain expertise during a time of transition. Maintaining established good practice was also identified as a key training and development issue for both Monitoring Officers (55% respondents) and members/officers more generally (71% respondents).

The new statutory duty to declare a pecuniary interest present an interesting question. One of the criticisms levelled against the previous framework was that the public adopted a 'there's no smoke without fire' approach to investigations, so that even if found innocent of a breach of the code any councillor will have her or his reputation tarnished. It remains to be seen what will happen to reputations once police investigations become the standard route for investigating councillors. What is certain is that Monitoring Officers once again felt that the legislation had not been expressed clearly enough, nor had been explained in a timely fashion. Eighty-seven per cent officers suggested that the new offence was not clear and one officer suggested:

> The DCLG support and guidance has been poor and there is still no definition of 'disclosable pecuniary interests' even though a number of Councils are aiming to take changes to their AGM's in May. There a number of decisions from DCLG which suggest they are 'minded' to change certain aspects of the legislation. This does not help with planning training and dissemination of information to a wide range of stakeholders. (Macaulay et al., 2012)

Ninety-two per cent respondents suggested that training is needed for Monitoring Officers in the new offence of failing to declare a pecuniary interest, whereas 95% also suggested that training is needed for Members and Officers in the new offence.

Finally the lack of sanctions was also seen as very worrying to Monitoring Officers. Eighty-eight per cent respondents thought that the new framework does not provide an adequate array of sanctions for misconduct and poor standards of behaviour. Views were expressed that a lack of sanctions would only lead to further public concern in the sense that any complaint may be seen as ultimately having nowhere to go. Such an argument is again very interesting considering the stated aim of the act to increase local participation and facilitate local empowerment: both of which are now arguably curbed in terms of transparency and integrity.

Perhaps even more worryingly some respondents were concerned about the possible perverse incentives that the new framework might generate:

> It will provide an incentive to try to resolve allegations informally or at the earliest possible stage of a formal process. However, there could be a perverse opposite incentive for some complainants to press allegations because the extent of 'damage' which might be done to a member will be limited. The problem area will be behavioural allegations which in fact are more serious because critics will be able to point to the potential cost and effort of investigation for little perceived outcome. (Macaulay et al., 2012, p. 5)

In terms of the integrity framework, then, the evidence suggests that major fault lines have opened up. Very recently, however, these have been widened and deepened further by the proposed reforms to local government accountability mechanisms.

A Pincer Movement on Integrity and Accountability?

It would be remiss to suggest that it was only the integrity system that has been subject to significant changes: local accountability structures are also due to be radically altered, again under the banner of localism. The 2013 Queen's Speech unveiled proposals for the *Local Audit and Accountability Bill*, which formally abolishes the Audit Commission and transfers its work to open competition in the private sector. The Department of Communities and Local Government (DCLG) suggests that this reform will encourage

> a more localist approach, giving local bodies the freedom to appoint their own auditors from an open and competitive market; manage their own audit arrangements, with appropriate safeguards to endure auditor independence; and retain the same high audit standards. (DCLG, 2013a, p. 4)

Yet the move to opening up public audit to private auditors has been met with fierce criticism, not because of any inherent flaw or inability in such firms but in the facts that it stands in stark contrast to the principle of auditors being independent of the audited body (DCLG Select Committee, 2011, p. 13). Even supporters of increased local control over audit processes and procedures have warned that without proper safeguards to protect independence any such policy could have 'disastrous' consequences on public trust (NLGN, 2011). In essence, the issue at stake is one of conflict of interest: can there be a genuinely independent audit of public sector organisations if the auditors are contracted by that organisation?

The key policies contained in the *Local Audit and Accountability Bill* have been strenuously debated since the abolition of the Audit Commission was announced in August 2010. Numerous reasons were given for this move. From an ideological point of view releasing decisions on audit to local authorities (and other bodies) was clearly within the mould of the localism agenda. There were also cost-saving issues: at the time it was originally announced that abolition of the Audit Commission would save approximately £50 million, a figure that was disputed by both the DCLG select committee and the Audit Commission itself (DCLG Select Committee, 2011, p. 11). Recent government figures suggest that the proposed Bill will deliver savings of £1.2 billion to the taxpayer, although this will be for savings across all policies contained in the bill, rather than simply the closure of the Audit Commission.

What immediately raised concern even in 2010 was that the alternative to the Audit Commission was the appointment of private auditors. The DCLG select committee showed that this contravened one of the fundamental principles of public audit that have existed since the 19th century and the *District Auditors Act 1879*. Principles of public audit has always differed from private sector audit, and along with the independence of public audit, other principles are that auditors may report widely to the public, councillors and other key stakeholders, and that their reporting also covers 'regularity' (legality), propriety (probity) and use of resources (value for money). These three principles were codified as recently as 1998 by the Public Audit Forum and restated again in the 2001 Sharman report (DCLG Select Committee, 2011, p. 13). Critics argue that the independence of auditors had been 'categorically established' (DCLG Select Committee, 2011, p. 14) and concerns were raised that the introduction of a local appointment process for auditors, without appropriate checks and balances, may result in conflicts of interests. A particular concern is the potential for a conflict between consultancy and audit services.

The independence of public audit is outlined in Part 3 of the Bill. Under Section 7, two or more auditors (who must be eligible under part 4 of the Bill) can be appointed to work independently or jointly once advice has been received by the Audit Panel. Under Section 8 all public bodies are to have an Audit Panel, with the exception of Chief Constables and the Commissioner of the Metropolitan Police. Its chief functions is to (1) advise the authority on the maintenance of an independent relationship with the local auditor appointed to audit its accounts (section 10 (1)), and to advise the authority on the selection and appointment of a local auditor to audit its accounts (section 10 (4))

In a welcome move, the majority of the Audit Panel must be independent and also be chaired by an independent member (Schedule 4 (1a and 1b)). In this case, an independent member is defined as follows.

> A member of a relevant authority's auditor panel, other than a health service body's auditor panel, is 'independent' at any given time if
>
> (a) the panel member has not been a member or officer of the authority within the period of 5 years ending with that time,
> (b) the panel member has not been an officer or employee of an entity connected with the authority within that period; and

(c) the panel member is not at that time a relative or close friend of a member or officer of the authority or an officer or employee of an entity connected with the authority.

This retention of an independent element is obviously important, but the key question is, will the Audit Panel protect the independence of the appointment process?

CONCLUSION

In a sense this chapter serves to flag up issues that – hopefully – will not arise in the future. The impact of the *Localism Act* and the *Local Audit and Accountability Bill* will not be felt for many years. It is not unreasonable to suggest, however, that legislative changes have opened up ethical fault lines in terms of integrity and accountability, and that these are a cause for concern.

So far the new integrity framework is not at all welcomed by local government officers. In our 2012 survey general perceptions of the new standards framework were, overwhelmingly, negative. The previous integrity framework was seen as flawed yet fulfilling an important role (Macaulay et al., 2010), and that in particular it had boosted public confidence in local government (Cowell et al., 2011). However 85% officers are not satisfied with the new framework and over two-thirds (67%) feel that the new framework is a step in the wrong direction for standards of conduct in local government. Seventy-nine per cent officers felt that the new framework is disproportionate in terms of its balance of rules and sanctions, whereas 68% do not think that the new framework will allow poor standards of conduct to be dealt with adequately. In addition the survey revealed a broad concern that the new standards framework will not have a positive impact on the public: 77% officers did not think that the new framework will improve public confidence in local government standards of conduct and 62% felt that it would have a negative impact on public trust.

The first fault line, then, is the general reaction. A second is the extra pressure placed on Monitoring Officers themselves. Previous research (Lawton, 1995) has already demonstrated the broad range of roles and functions undertaken by these officers and it has been left to them to implement the new framework. Unsurprisingly Monitoring Officers have felt under-resourced and perceive a lack of support from central government:

> In terms of Orders or Regulations from Central Government on the recruitment of Independent Persons. I have been asking for this by phone and email since early April

> – and this has not materialised. We had seen a letter to an MP in the north of England stating that we may be able to use the existing independent lay members – but nothing has come to all Councils, as it should. This is simply unacceptable. Guidance from DCLG is non-existent. (Macaluay et al., 2012, p. 8)

These reactions can be understood fairly easily in terms of the Integrity Management System (IMS) model (Maesschalck & Bertok, 2009), which identifies further fault lines. Application of the IMS model suggests that the new framework is substantially weaker than the previous version. In terms of *defining* integrity, the new version of the code is perceived as potentially more vague and unhelpful (as is the legislation more generally). *Leading* integrity has suffered: the strategic regulator has been abolished; the local standards committee has gone; the replacement, an independent person, does not seem to have a leadership role and even if she or he did, the legislation remains unclear as to how the person will work within an authority. *Monitoring* integrity remains the least touched as registers of interest are still required, although there are no longer any statutory requirements under the Act for a gifts and hospitality register (although it seems difficult to think that these will not be maintained on a voluntary basis). *Enforcing* integrity is much more difficult because local sanctions have been removed and it remains to be seen what type of impact new offence of failing to declare an interest may have.

The movement away from such well-established, and hitherto relatively uncontested, principles of public audit leads to even more concerns, and another critical fault line in the governance arrangements of English local government. One final issue is that both the *Localism Act 2011* and *Local Audit and Accountability Bill* intend, on a very broad level, to promote local decision-making at the most appropriate level. It is a curious thing, therefore, that so many opportunities for local authorities to monitor and govern their own behaviour have been substantially decreased and perhaps indicates that local government in England continues to be local only at the behest of Westminster. As stated previously, only the future will tell us whether or not these new governance arrangements have any positive or negative impacts. Yet the concerns about them have already been clearly expressed and one hopes that they can be addressed before the fault lines in English local government create an ethical earthquake that engulfs the regime.

REFERENCES

Communities and Local Government Committee. (2011). *Audit and inspection of local authorities*. Fourth Report of Session. HM Government, London.

Committee on Standards in Public Life. (1997). *Third report on the committee for standards in public life: Standards of conduct in local government in England, Scotland and Wales*, Cm3702. London: TSO.

Committee on Standards in Public Life. (2005). *Tenth report on the committee for standards in public life: Getting the balance right implementing standards of conduct in public life*, Cm6407. London: TSO.

Cowell, R. I., Downe, J., & Morgan, K. (2011). The ethical framework for Local government in England: Is it having any effect and why? *Public Management Review, 13*(3), 433–457.

de Graaf, G., & van der Wal, Z. (2010). Managing conflicting public values: Governing with integrity and effectiveness. *American Review of Public Administration, 40*(6), 623–630.

Department for Communities and Local Government. (2013). *Local audit and accountability bill: A plain english guide*. HM Government, London.

Department for Communities and Local Government. (2005). *Standards of conduct in local government: the Future*. HM Government, London.

Evans, M. (2012). Beyond the integrity paradox – towards 'good enough' governance?. *Policy Studies, 33*(1), 97–113.

Head, B. W. (2012). The contribution of integrity agencies to good governance. *Policy Studies, 33*(1), 7–20.

Head, B. W., Brown, A. J., & Connors, C. (Eds.). (2008). *Promoting integrity: Evaluating and improving public institutions*. Farnham, Surrey: Ashgate.

Huberts, L., Anechiarico, F., & Six, F. (Eds.). (2008). *Local integrity systems: World cities fighting corruption and safeguarding integrity*. The Hague: BJU Publishers.

Jennings, M. (2006). *The seven signs of ethical collapse*. New York, NY: St. Martin's Griffin.

Keohane, N., Roth, O., Hildyard, L., & Mehta, S. (2011). *Show me the money accounting for localism*. London: New local Government Network.

Lawton, A., Iles, P., Llewellyn, N., Macaulay, M., & Thompson, B. (2005). *Supporting monitoring officers*. London: Standards Board for England.

Lawton, A., & Macaulay, M. (2005). *Analysis of the code of conduct consultation*. London: Standards Board for England.

Lawton, A., & Macaulay, M. (2009). *Notable practice in standards committees*. Manchester: Standards for England.

Local Government and Public Involvement in Health Act. (2007). Part 10: Ethical standards.

Macaulay, M., Hickey, G., & Begum, N. (2012). *Preparing for the new standards regime in English local government*. Middlesbrough: University of Teesside.

Macaulay, M, Hickey, G., & Newman, C. (2010). *The local integrity system in the UK*. Paper presented at the European Group for Public Administration (EGPA) Annual Conference, Toulouse.

Macaulay, M., Newman, C., Lucas, R., & Peake, S. (2010). *Comparing standards frameworks*. Manchester: Standards for England.

Maesschalck, J., & Bertok, J. (2009). *Towards a sound integrity framework: Instruments, processes, structures and conditions for implementation*. Paris: OECD Global Forum on Public Governance.

Matei, A., Matei, L., & Savulescu, C. (2010). Public integrity, economic freedom and governance performance. A comparative study for the EU member states and acceding countries. *Theoretical and Applied Economics, XVII.11*(552), 21–52.

Office of the Deputy Prime Minister. (2005). *The role and effectiveness of the Standards Board for England*, HC 60-1. London: TSO.

Sampford, C., Smith, R., & Brown, A. J. (2005). From Greek temple to bird's nest: Towards a theory of coherence and mutual accountability for national integrity systems. *Australian Journal of Public Administration*, *64*(2).

Salminen, A., Ikola-Norrbacka, R., & Rinna, H. (2009). Trust and integrity violations in Finnish public administration: The views of citizens. *Hulduskultuur*, *10*, 74–93.

Transparency International (TI). (2012). *National Integrity System background rationale and methodology* Retrieved from http://www.transparency.org/files/content/nis/NIS_Background_Methodology_EN.pdf

Trevino, L. K., Brown, M., & Hartman, L. P. (2003). A qualitative investigation of perceived executive ethical leadership: Perceptions from inside and outside the executive suite. *Human Relations*, *56*, 5.

RETHINKING URBAN REGENERATION? INSIGHTS INTO THE FUTURE THROUGH USE OF THE STRATEGIC-RELATIONAL APPROACH

Simon Pemberton

ABSTRACT

Purpose – *The chapter summarises issues associated with the effectiveness of urban policy interventions. In particular it emphasises the importance of sites, scales and spaces of state activity and the implications for the current and future nature of regeneration governance, policy and practice.*

Methodology/approach – *The chapter draws upon strategic-relational state theory.*

Findings – *With reference to the United Kingdom (UK), there are significant changes taking place that are affecting the site, scale and nature of urban regeneration. However, there is considerable uncertainty over*

Looking for Consensus?: Civil Society, Social Movements and Crises for Public Management
Critical Perspectives on International Public Sector Management, Volume 2, 45–58

ISSN: 2045-7944/doi:10.1108/S2045-7944(2013)0000002004

the extent to which discrepancies in performance between *areas will be addressed.*

Research implications – *Further research will be required on the consequences for regeneration of the rescaling of state power, the changing institutions of the state and the emergence of new political forces and strategies.*

Originality/value of the chapter – *The chapter provides a theoretical and empirical framework to understand both the current and future nature of urban regeneration governance in the UK and beyond.*

Keywords: Urban regeneration; governance; state theory

INTRODUCTION

The rise of globalisation, post-industrialism, and associated processes of deindustrialisation and de-urbanisation have had a significant impact on the evolving nature of cities in the United Kingdom (UK) and beyond (Tallon, 2010). In response, there has been increasing recognition of the new state institutions and associated forms of urban governance that have emerged to deliver urban regeneration. These can be located within a wider shift from 'urban managerialism' to 'urban entrepreneurialism' (Harvey, 1989), as well as in relation to the changing spaces and scales of state activity (Mahon & Keil, 2009).

Nevertheless, such a reconstitution is not wholly surprising given that 'the rescaling of governance and the production of new state spaces is an on-going and highly contested process' (Brenner, 2004, p. 76), and that 'state scalar structures are now understood to be historically malleable: they may be ruptured and rewoven by the very political strategies they enable' (*ibid.* 2009, p. 126). Consequently – and based upon such an appreciation – we can begin to generate a more nuanced insight of the implications for urban policy and the discourse and practice of 'urban regeneration' that emerged both in the UK and beyond from the early 1990s.

Indeed, whilst Roberts and Sykes (2000)' seminal *Urban Regeneration: A Handbook* viewed urban regeneration as a technical process, there was less conceptual discussion of the changing form and governance of urban regeneration, nor on the influence of the state and/or other social forces and political–territorial alliances therein. Nevertheless, such issues have been increasingly recognised in respect of their importance; for example, Cochrane (2007) has focussed on the ways in which urban policy has been managed – and on whose terms – whilst recent work by Cox (2010) has alerted us to the importance of the 'politics of scale' and the importance of political strategy in shaping the rescaling of state interventions and the implications for structures and networks of (regeneration) governance.

This is important given the collapse of the global financial markets in 2007, which exposed traditional property-led regeneration models as being largely unsustainable. Indeed, coupled with increasing public austerity measures in an era of considerable economic turbulence, there has been a paradigmatic shift in both the process and delivery of regeneration within the UK and beyond. In essence, the era of the state underwriting regeneration activity – certainly in the context of the UK – has passed and there is now an increasing concern with decentralising responsibility and activity to a wider range of stakeholders – including local communities – to deliver new forms of regeneration (Department for Communities and Local Government (DCLG), 2011). But in turn, this raises new and important questions over the institutions, actors and scales that may be privileged and the influence of the state and other political interests therein.

Within this broad context, this chapter draws upon strategic-relational state theory and the strategic-relational approach (SRA) (Jessop, 2008, 1997) to explore both current and future prospects for urban regeneration governance, policy and practice. In essence, the SRA helps to draw our attention to how the changing institutions and geography of the state can influence the nature of political strategies and how these may subsequently influence urban regeneration governance and policy. But equally, it also draws our attention to the dialectical relationship that exists in that we additionally need to understand how local political strategies themselves can inform the changing institutions and geography of the state (Pemberton & Goodwin, 2010). In the context of urban regeneration what this means is that it becomes possible to locate new forms and scales of urban regeneration governance – for example, the shift under the coalition government to sub-regional and localist approaches in England – within wider sets of social and political forces that may mediate/influence the reconfiguration of state power. Moreover, the use of the SRA helps us to understand how new objects of governance for urban regeneration may be formed by social and political forces operating at specific scales and through specific strategies. Again, this is important if reference is made to the current restructuring taking place under the coalition government in England and the introduction (for example) of elected mayors, enterprise zones and sub-regional Local Enterprise Partnerships (LEPs). Indeed, in this respect, the SRA also provides useful insights into how contemporary and future structural changes in the institutions and actors responsible for the governance of urban regeneration (such as those listed above) can impact on the strategies that are subsequently pursued (and vice versa). Finally, the approach also helps to highlight the ways in which the new institutions and political actors that emerge in the context of urban regeneration may define particular territorial spaces for intervention based around their activities, and how these are promoted and embedded by those who are politically powerful.

PROBLEMATIZING URBAN REGENERATION, THE STATE AND LOCAL SOCIAL AND POLITICAL FORCES

Looking back to Furbey's (1999) discussion on the metaphor of 'regeneration', a key point that he makes – and which continues to resonate more than 10 years later – is that 'regeneration seems to offer an almost infinitely inclusive canopy under which all may be persuaded to shelter and find agreement, yet vital issues remain beyond the pale' (1999, p. 440). This is reflected in terms of the varying emphases placed by successive governments and policy makers on '*physical regeneration*', '*economic regeneration*' and/or '*neighbourhood/social*' regeneration (Tallon, 2010).

But perhaps more importantly, it is the latter point that Furbey makes with regards to issues that appear to be less emphasised or prioritised that is crucial: in his paper he suggests that regeneration's strongest connections appear to be with individualistic and statist traditions (p. 440) and consequently there has been little attention placed on 'the actions of the excluders and addressing fundamental issues of power' (p. 441). Hence it is perhaps unsurprising to note that in the UK those critical of the previous governments' emphasis on a 'third way' approach have pointed out that too much emphasis was placed on physical and economic regeneration to secure private commercial wealth generation at the expense of welfare/wealth redistribution (Diamond, Liddle, Southern, & Osei 2010). Furthermore, this concern with securing economic competitiveness and the 'hiving off' of neighbourhood regeneration into a separate discourse and practice of renewal has arguably compounded the lack of attention on who wins and who loses from physical/economic approaches (Cameron, 2003).

If a wider European perspective is taken, evidence from other regeneration schemes in Europe has highlighted how issues of scale and the rescaling of regeneration governance are also important in illuminating the importance of politics and associated issues of power – and how outcomes may reflect the political strategies of the dominant forces (such as the state) prompting rescaling, as well as those contesting/resisting such moves (Cox, 2010). Thus recent moves by a number of EU governments (e.g. France, the Netherlands) to emphasise city-regional/poly-centric approaches in order to target social housing suburbs in the urban periphery – and which can pose some of the greatest regeneration challenges – are arguably welcome given that Tallon (2010) has highlighted the relative overemphasis in previous urban policy on meeting the needs of inner-city (business) elites at the expense of the outer suburbs.

In the UK, Valler and Carpenter (2010) note that under the previous New Labour government (1997–2010), the initial emphasis on sub-national economic governance was rather incoherent – both in respect of ideological foundation and policy approach. Indeed, despite the emergence of devolved governance in Scotland, Wales and Northern Ireland and the introduction of Regional Development Agencies (RDAs) in England, attempts at decentralisation were again informed around the role of place in driving competitiveness. In turn, they suggest that this impacted upon the level of political commitment and durability of the regional approach, and whilst the failure of the regional referendum in North-East England in 2004 led to the emergence of a sub-regional agenda, this remained ad hoc in nature due to the absence of a clear ideological drive (*ibid.*).

Coupled with the post-2007 credit crunch and subsequent economic recession, what can be discerned more broadly is the fact that the coherence and nature of urban regeneration policy reflects both the political (discourses) and ideological persuasion of the government in power, as well as the broader economic context. In turn, this then shapes the key sites, scales, strategies and structures promoted for urban regeneration and those privileged therein. Moreover, whilst the current coalition government in the UK lacked an explicit regeneration programme whilst in opposition, since its election in 2010 it has recently delivered a review of *Regeneration to Enable Growth* (DCLG, 2011). This acknowledges that 'the accepted physical regeneration model of the late 1990s and early 2000s financed on the back of cheap credit, increased land values and high-density residential development has been severely undermined by current financial and economic conditions' (Glossop, 2009, p. 63). As a result, it sets out its ambitions for promoting locally driven growth and encouraging business investment through a more permissive approach in order to rebalance the economy (one-third of employees in Northern England are currently in public-sector employment). It also seeks to promote economic development through a more decentralised approach and through different models of finance. But as we shall see through use of the SRA, whilst this may lead to a more tailored and flexible system, it may also contribute to the marginalisation and disempowerment of certain actors and interests.

Such issues have indeed been raised in a House of Commons Communities and Local Government Select Committee Report 2011 on regeneration, and which suggested that 'Regeneration to Enable Growth' needed to be clearer in its approach, both in terms of what it actually means by the term 'regeneration', the problems it is trying to solve (and for whom) and to what overall outcomes the measures set out will contribute. In response, the coalition government has re-affirmed its localist approach and argued that it is for local partners to develop their own regeneration strategies in order to address their own priorities (Department for Communities and Local Government (DCLG), 2012, p. 5). However, such capacities and capabilities of local partners may vary and it could prove to be more difficult to address economic and social problems in certain areas of the country, for example in small- and medium-sized cities dependent on single declining economic sectors that have suffered the most from the recent recession in the UK (Centre for Cities, 2009).

THE SRA AS A TOOL TO EXPLORE THE FUTURE NATURE OF URBAN REGENERATION

Given the apparent lack of emphasis on national redistributive strategies to address socio-spatial economic inequalities (Shaw & Robinson, 2010), it is therefore pertinent to explore how the new sites, scales and spaces of state activity that are emerging in the UK (and England more specifically) can influence the future nature of urban regeneration, and the subsequent extent to which these types of inequalities are either ameliorated or exacerbated.

The SRA – as a non-functionalist account – can assist in this respect. It has been identified as 'perhaps the most theoretically sophisticated discussion of the state currently available' (Kelly, 1999, p. 109). In this respect, it has been used in a variety of different contexts: for example, Valler and Wood (2004) explored the response of business interests to the rise of

English regionalism under New Labour through the SRA lens and highlighted how it helped to generate a better understanding of how on-going centralism – as well as the perceptions and organisation of business interests – impinged on the relatively limited restructuring of business activity that took place. Lagendijk (2007) has also drawn on the SRA to make the point that local social and political forces can influence the nature and form of city-regionalism and the areas/interests privileged. This finding segues into Brenner's argument that the SRA's 'theoretical linchpin' is centred on the notion of how political strategies – and actors therein – influence state form and structure and how changes in state structures help to produce changes in political strategies.

There are three key points in relation the SRA. First, the state should be viewed in relational terms: the power of the state is the power of the social and political forces acting in and through the state, such as state managers, regional interests and so forth – that is, 'the peopled state' (Jessop, 1990, pp. 269–270). But the state is more permeable to certain social and political forces than others and any territorial restructuring is therefore likely to impact on the shape and power of these forces over time and space. So the social and political forces that can gain access to new institutions associated with the governance of urban regeneration (for example) will vary depending on the scale and nature of such institutions being considered.

Second, the existence of the state as a distinct social relation does not guarantee the delivery of a particular set of activities: the coherence of the state is created through particular (hegemonic) projects and activities focused around particular agendas. Such (hegemonic) projects and agendas are promoted by different social and political forces that are then able to develop and implement a series of political strategies at the local level. Consequently, as structures for governing urban regeneration change, so too will the dominant social and political forces and the political strategies that are pursued. In essence, those political and social forces that are able to act 'in and through' the state will seek to develop a range of political strategies that are then used by civil servants and politicians to 'harness state institutions towards particular socio-economic projects' (Brenner, 2004, p. 87).

Third, the state is 'strategically' and 'spatially' selective: certain types of political strategy are favoured by the state over others. As a result, particularly powerful (hegemonic) groups may exert more power than others and the state may therefore privilege their strategies, interests, coalitions, spatial scales of action and time horizons over others (Jessop, 1997, p. 53). Nevertheless, such strategies and their implementation are influenced themselves by 'spatial imaginaries' and hence the actions of the dominant social and political forces are important in generating ideas and narratives conducive to particular types of intervention required over a particular space. But once again, such imaginaries that can be used to construct different types of projects and 'objects of governance' will change too as the structures of the state change (Pemberton & Goodwin, 2010).

From a methodological and practical perspective, we can apply this approach to help develop new insights into the changing nature of regeneration governance, policy and practice in the UK and elsewhere. Nevertheless, this initial discussion is confined to England because the UK state continues to govern England in a highly centralised way, arguably in marked contrast to the devolution of authority to Scotland, Wales and Northern Ireland (Pike & Tomaney, 2009).

First, the SRAs stress on political strategies and state projects draws our attention to whether different 'objects of governance' will be created as new structures of governance emerge for urban regeneration. These may be underpinned by new political strategies and state projects that emerge, and which are promoted by the dominant social and political forces operating at different scales. In the context of England, it is clear from both the coalition government's review of *Regeneration to Enable Growth* (DCLG, 2011), and its response to the House of Commons Communities and Local Government Select Committee Report (2011) on Regeneration that an economic/business competitiveness agenda is predominating, and this is also being informed by the new structures, strategies and scales of working that have emerged. For example, the Regional Development Agencies (RDAs) and Regional Assemblies (RAs) that were set up under the previous government have now been abolished. But these have been replaced by LEPs which have a primary economic function and which have a strong private-sector presence on their management boards. Furthermore, the fact that many responsibilities previously allocated to the regional level have currently been centralised within Whitehall (such as inward investment and European funding) means that they have a narrower focus on business and entrepreneurial support, although admittedly this may change following the allocation of the next tranche of European structural funds in 2014.

The regional government offices in England that were set up in 1994 have also disappeared, although in London the abolition of the London Development Agency (LDA) has led to the transfer of its city-wide regeneration powers and the management of European funding to the Greater London Authority (GLA) and an increasingly powerful Mayor (Cook, 2010). This again has implications for the relationship between the state, those politically powerful at a local scale and the objects of governance for urban regeneration (as well as their potential rescaling) that are promoted by the state institutions that remain, such as the GLA. For example, the expansion of responsibilities for the GLA over housing (through devolving powers over housing investment from the Homes and Communities Agency) and economic development may – on the one hand – have led to a similar emphasis – as per previous arrangements – upon local employment and skills programmes, as well as 'job brokerage' activities. However, it appears that an alternative strategy is emerging that involves financial cuts in some of these areas and a greater emphasis being placed on market-led provision and a narrower set of economic objectives focused on stimulating entrepreneurial activity/business competitiveness. It also appears that certain parts of the capital – such as East London and out into the Thames Gateway area – are being privileged over other areas through the mayor being given new powers to create Mayoral Development Corporations to secure East London's Olympic legacy (Cook, 2010; HM Government, 2010).

In addition, the increased emphasis on local authorities for facilitating and delivering regeneration activity by the coalition government (Lawless, 2010) highlights how new social and political forces are also emerging at the local level. It appears that some of these are now attempting to facilitate LEP activity in conjunction with the private sector in order to take forward and implement particular strategies and policies. But this will be at the expense of other strategies and policies associated with social and political forces that become less dominant.

Other commentators have also noted that the *Decentralisation and Localism Act* passed in November 2011 will lead to contradictions emerging in respect of policy priorities for urban regeneration. For instance, the General Power of Competence for local authorities allows them to do anything apart from that which is specifically prohibited. However, on the other hand the Act provides a new right for communities to shape their local areas through the development of neighbourhood plans but which should also generally conform to existing plans and policies (HM Government, 2010, 2011). Consequently, how this plays out in practice remains uncertain but it is clear that there will be variation emerging across England in respect of the eventual balance/privileging of regeneration strategies/policies being promoted at different scales of governance.

Second, the SRA can also be used to explore how structural changes in the institutions responsible for the governance of urban regeneration will impact on the strategies and projects that are subsequently pursued by the dominant social and political forces (and vice versa). Here, the construction of particular 'hegemonic projects' that seek to mobilise cultural and ideological support behind particular programmes of activity can help to resolve conflicts between different interests (albeit often temporally and unevenly). Under the previous Conservative administration in the UK (1979–1997) MacKinnon (2001) argues that what we arguably witnessed were national hegemonic projects emphasising enterprise, neo-liberalism and personal responsibility and which promoted the interests of business (e.g. through creation of unelected agencies) over and above those of trade unions and local authorities.

Such projects were modified to an extent under the previous New Labour government in the UK, who espoused a 'third way' ideology focused on a mixed economy of provision involving public–private partnerships, participatory democracy and a 'new localism' (Imrie & Raco, 2003) focused around a deficit model of communities (Diamond & Liddle, 2005).

But what we can now discern are new strategic and spatial selectivities and new forms of political and moral leadership emerging under the new coalition government. These are potentially beginning to privilege certain regeneration 'communities' over others, and the power of the dominant social and political forces.

From a spatial perspective, in contrast to the previous Conservative administration (1979–1997) the coalition government has launched a *Regional Growth Fund* focused on stimulating private investment, and it has stated that it will 'not allow the great North–South divide to reappear'. Hence it is 'giving (funding) emphasis to areas with the most problems – the North-East, North-West, Yorkshire and the Humber, and the West Midlands' (Vince Cable, Business Secretary, quoted in Cook, 2010). Nevertheless, such a budget is small when compared to the budgets commanded by the RDAs. In addition, the fact that the state will be less involved in directly underwriting future regeneration activity means that the divergence in economic performance and prospects for urban regeneration between London and the rest of the UK is likely to persist. In essence, we may witness an on-going spatial selectivity focused around maintaining London's (and the South-East) competitive advantage through economic imperatives, rather than on seriously addressing national socio-spatial economic inequalities.

From a strategic perspective, with the coalition government scrapping the RDAs in England and with an emphasis now being placed on elected mayors – as well as local government and local communities to develop new approaches to tackling local regeneration problems – it is possible that such interests may supplant those of the private sector, and with benefits accruing to a broader social base. However, on the other hand, the introduction of Enterprise Zones (EZs), the establishment of LEPs and the emphasis on more permissive entrepreneurial activity arguably points towards the strategic privileging of private-sector interests over and above other actors.

Finally, the SRA can also be used to draw our attention to the ways in which the actions of new institutions and political actors that emerge in the context of urban regeneration may lead to the development of new governance arrangements that have both a different territorial and relational expression. In turn, associated questions arise over which actors are the dominant forces, and how such dominance is expressed. Hence, with reference to changes now taking place in the context of England, it is clear that those involved in both the existing and new structures of governance emerging for urban regeneration will be re-defining their territorial scales of working as new coalitions/partnerships emerge. This will not be straightforward given the plethora of governance mechanisms already in place for urban regeneration. For example, Pike and Tomaney (2009) point out that at least seven spatial entities have recently emerged for urban regeneration activity following the faltering of the regionalisation project by the previous Government.

Such arrangements are likely to become even more complex over the next few years given the fact that LEPs in England are based upon 'functional economic areas', and with 6 of the 39 LEPs that now cover England having core geographies that overlap previous regional administrative boundaries. Furthermore, there has been a preference within central government for city-regional/sub-regional partnerships that evolved under earlier governance arrangements to be incorporated under LEP structures. Indeed, this has been the case in areas such as Leeds and Merseyside. But if LEPs are to succeed in delivering certain types of services and infrastructure they will also need to combine and work over broader (regional) territories. This subsequently raises important questions over the extent to which actors will be able to work coherently and effectively together to shape appropriate governance structures and policy outcomes. Indeed, to what extent will endogenous regeneration strategies at a sub-regional level seek to promote the interests of a selective group of individuals, such as city mayors? Will this make it more difficult to construct partnerships that operate over a wider territorial scale, and which seek to interact with regional and/or national level institutions?

CONCLUSIONS

Through use of the SRA framework, the chapter begins to respond to a call by Neil Brenner (2009) for more concrete research into the scale differentiation and subsequent rescaling of specific state policies and associated institutions, as well as the evolvement of such processes.

From a theoretical and empirical perspective it highlights how future forms of urban regeneration governance, policy and practice need to be understood in the context of the changing nature of state institutions – and perhaps crucially – the changing nature of local political strategy. It then becomes possible to understand how new objects of governance may emerge in particular places, at particular times and across varying territorial scales according to the predominant social and political forces at work. In this sense, whilst the chapter focused predominantly on England, there is no reason why the SRA conceptual approach could not be used elsewhere too.

Moving beyond initial discussions that identified the need for greater clarity over what we mean by 'urban regeneration', the use of the SRA indicated that what we are now seeing in England is a new period of strategic and spatial selectivity. It is rather early to speculate on whether the new structures and policies emerging for urban regeneration in England will address pre-existing socio-spatial economic inequalities. However, it is clear that care will be required in respect of the new objects of governance that are promoted and their ability to address such issues, the scope of hegemonic projects that emerge and the benefits that subsequently accrue to a broad(er) social base and the prioritisation of spatial selectivities that ameliorate, rather than exacerbate discrepancies in performance both between and within areas. Working through the governance of complexity will also be crucial for those involved in the new structures of governance that emerge so that they can effectively demarcate a space amenable to particular forms of intervention. This latter point is important as Pike and Tomaney (2009) note that fragmentation and incoherence have afflicted the governance of urban regeneration to date and which they feel has negative implications for the ability of any future structures and strategies for urban regeneration addressing uneven development and territorial equity and justice.

Nevertheless, we do need to be careful that we do not imply that the central state can fix problems per se through creating new structures for governing and delivering urban regeneration. As noted already, the exact nature of governance will be dependent on the range of social and political forces operating at a variety of scales in and through the state (also see Pemberton & Goodwin, 2010). The example from London neatly encapsulates this point, with the abolition of the LDA illustrating the constant interplay between state structure and (local) political strategy, and the subsequent forms of urban governance that may emerge and evolve.

REFERENCES

Brenner, N. (2004). *New state spaces: Urban governance and the rescaling of statehood*. Oxford: Oxford University Press.

Brenner, N. (2009). Open questions of state rescaling. *Cambridge Journal of Regions, Economy and Society*, *2*, 123–139.

Cameron, S. (2003). Gentrification, housing re-differentiation and urban regeneration: 'Going for growth' in Newcastle-upon-Tyne. *Urban Studies*, *40*(12), 2367–2382.

Centre for Cities. (2009). *Cities Outlook 2009*, Centre for Cities, London.

Cochrane, A. (2007). *Understanding urban policy. A critical approach*. Oxford: Blackwell.

Cook, B. (2010). *Coalition 'won't allow north-south divide to reappear'*. Retrieved from www.regen.net. Accessed on 14 June 2010.

Cox, K. (2010). The problem of metropolitan governance and the politics of scale. *Regional Studies*, *44*(2), 215–227.

Department for Communities and Local Government (DCLG). (2012). *Government response to the house of commons communities and local government committee report of session 2010–12: Regeneration*. London: DCLG.

Department for Communities and Local Government (DCLG). (2011). *Regeneration to enable growth: What government is doing in support of community-led regeneration*. London: DCLG.

Diamond, J., & Liddle, J. (2005). *The management of regeneration*. Abingdon: Routledge.

Diamond, J., Liddle, J., Southern, A., & Osei, P. (Eds.). (2010). *Urban regeneration management: International perspectives*. Abingdon: Routledge.

Furbey, R. (1999). Urban 'regeneration': Reflections on a metaphor. *Critical Social Policy*, *19*(4), 419–445.

Glossop, C. (2009). Regenertating cities. In P. Hackett, (Ed.), *Regeneration in a downturn: What needs to change?* (pp. 62–67). London: The Smith Institute.

Harvey, D. (1989). From managerialism to entrepreneurialism: the transformation of urban governance in late capitalism. *Geografiska Annaler*, *71B*, 3–17.

HM Government. (2011). *Decentralisation and Localism Act*. London: DCLG.

HM Government. (2010). *Decentralisation and the Localism Bill: An essential guide*. London: DCLG.

House of Commons Communities and Local Government Select Committee. (2011). *Committee report of session 2010–12: Regeneration*. London: DCLG.

Imrie, R., & Raco, M. (2003). Community and the changing nature of urban policy. In R. Imrie, & M. Raco (Eds.), *Urban renaissance? New labour, community and urban policy* (pp. 3–36). Bristol: The Policy Press.

Jessop, B. (1990). *State theory: Putting the capitalist state in its place*. Cambridge: Polity Press.

Jessop, B. (1997). A neo-gramscian approach to the regulation of urban regimes. In M. Lauria (Ed.), *Reconstructing urban regime theory: Regulating urban politics in a global economy* (pp. 51–73). London: Sage.

Jessop, B. (2008). *State power: A strategic relational approach*. Cambridge: Polity Press.

Kelly, D. (1999) The strategic-relational view of the state. *Politics*, *19*(2), 109–115.

Lagendijk, A. (2007). The accident of the region: A strategic relational perspective on the construction of the region's significance. *Regional Studies*, *41*(9), 1193–1208.

Lawless, P. (2010). Urban Regeneration: Is there a future? *People, Place and Policy Online*, *4*(1), 24–28.

Mackinnon, D. (2001). Regulating regional spaces: state agencies and the production of governance in the Scottish Highlands. *Environment and Planning A*, *33*(5), 823–844.

Mahon, R., & Keil, R. (Eds.). (2009). *Leviathan Undone? Towards a political economy of scale*. Vancouver: UBC Press.

Pemberton, S., & Goodwin, M. (2010). State power, local government reorganisation and accumulation and hegemony in the countryside. *Journal of Rural Studies*, *26*(3), 272–283.

Pike, A., & Tomaney, J. (2009). The state and uneven development: The governance of economic development in England in the post-devolution UK. *Cambridge Journal of Regions, Economy and Society*, *2*, 13–34.

Roberts, P., & Sykes, H. (2000). *Urban Regeneration: A handbook*. London: Sage.

Shaw, K., & Robinson, F. (2010). UK urban regeneration policies in the early twenty-first century continuity or change? *Town Planning Review*, *81*(2), 123–149.

Tallon, A. (2010). *Urban Regeneration in the UK*. London: Routledge.

Valler, D., & Carpenter, J. (2010). New labour's spaces of competitiveness. *Local Economy*, *25*(5-6), 438–456.

Valler, D., & Wood, A. (2004). Devolution and the politics of business representation in Britain: a strategic-relational approach. *Environment and Planning A*, *36*(10), 1835–1854.

THE RETREAT OF THE STATE: THE CHALLENGES FACED BY REGENERATION MANAGERS IN A CLIMATE OF AUSTERITY ☆

Lee Pugalis and David McGuinness

ABSTRACT

Purpose of this chapter – *A climate of austerity has gripped the politico-economic philosophy of many nation states across Europe and beyond as governments seek to rebalance budget deficits. This presents unique challenges for those engaged in purposeful acts aiming to regenerate communities of places – the regeneration managers.*

Design/methodology/approach – *England provides an interesting case study to examine some of the prime challenges facing regeneration managers by focusing on the ideologies that have informed successive UK governments' policy responses and spatial strategies. The main body of research, including interviews, was carried out between 2010 and 2012, and was subsequently updated in early 2013.*

☆This chapter is updated and adapted from the paper 'From a framework to a toolkit: Urban regeneration in an age of austerity', published in the *Journal of Urban Regeneration and Renewal*, 6(4), 339–353. ISSN 1752-9638.

Looking for Consensus?: Civil Society, Social Movements and Crises for Public Management
Critical Perspectives on International Public Sector Management, Volume 2, 59–85

ISSN: 2045-7944/doi:10.1108/S2045-7944(2013)0000002005

Findings – *Tracing an apparent transmutation of urban regeneration policy, the chapter helps to unmask a spatially unjust neoliberal toolkit, albeit pierced by some socially motivated actually existing regeneration initiatives. The transmutation of regeneration that has taken place is often concealed by de facto austerity measures and austerity politics.*

Research limitations – *The programme of interviews remains ongoing, as the research continues to track the shifting contours of state-led regeneration policy. Analysis is therefore provisional and explorative, with more detailed research reports and publications subject to follow.*

Practical implications – *The chapter explores emerging new agendas and sets out to identify some of the primary challenges that regeneration managers must face.*

Social implications – *'Regeneration' as a state-led policy objective and political concern has been virtually expunged from the Coalition lexicon. The present policy preference is to target public resources in 'value-added' schemes that favour private oriented objectives in a highly unbalanced way.*

What is original/value of paper – *The curtailment of broader regeneration debates has framed discussions limited to the depth of cuts, the speed of implementation and the spatial distribution of such measures. The result is that regeneration, understood as a capitalist policy instrument intended to respond to and assuage the outcomes produced by capitalist frameworks, is no more.*

Keywords: Austerity; Coalition Government; incentives regeneration; Labour Government; single-minded economic growth

INTRODUCTION

Urban regeneration programmes and area-based initiatives can be distinguished from other public policies because of their geographic focus. That is to say that particular places are designated for special forms of state assistance beyond the norm, i.e. urban regeneration sites. Although not always referred to as regeneration, such special assistance has been a defining feature of state policies around the world from the 1940s onwards: whether upgrading slum conditions in Bogotá or revitalising the post-industrial waterfronts of Boston, MA. Certainly not beyond criticism in conceptual terms, specific regeneration practices – from estate renewal to the renaissance of commercial quarters – continue to generate heated public debate and raise some fundamental political questions. Yet, a mainstay of urban regeneration theory and discourse has been its explicit or implicit aim to ameliorate some of the social, economic and environmental injustices produced by capitalist modes of production, namely uneven patterns of development. Rae observes that area-based regeneration programmes 'have been, and continue to be, a major weapon in the government armoury when dealing with urban decay' (Rae, 2011, p. 331).

Over the past four decades in the case of countries such as the United Kingdom and the United States, but more recently for other countries such as China, public policies have, in broad terms, shifted from redistribution towards more market enabling approaches consistent with neoliberal political outlooks. Nevertheless, the variegated forms and effects of actually existing neoliberalisation need to be acknowledged. Thus, according to Jamie Peck, the fiscal purging of recurrent neoliberal acts has resulted 'in the cumulative incapacitation of the state' (Peck, 2012). This would imply that the current age of austerity presents considerable challenges for holistically framed patterns of regeneration that many communities of need around the world grew accustomed to over the past two decades. A key question arises from the retreat of the welfare state: what are the challenges facing regeneration managers? Yet, recent empirically informed research, which may help to reveal some of the actually existing patterns of austerity-induced regeneration, has been noticeably lacking. There is a critical gap in knowledge of the framings of English regeneration since the UK General Election in 2010, partly because of a renewed and all-encompassing political discourse of 'localism' (Bentley & Pugalis, 2013). In addition, a political discourse of fiscal purging that pervades a climate of austerity promotes a local 'growth' narrative. Critical analyses that seek to excavate whether a transmutation in state-led regeneration policies has actually materialised or whether such a shift has been focused on appearance or the substantive form of regeneration have remained largely unexplored.[1] It is these issues that framed the research project reported in this chapter.

BACKDROP

UK governments have a long history of experimenting with a range of area-based mechanisms, such as the New Town Development Corporations in the late 1940s and Community Development Projects in the 1970s. However, it was legislation by Thatcher's Conservative Government that paved the way for a range of market-oriented regeneration ventures, including Urban Development Corporations (UDCs) and Enterprise Zones (EZs) in the 1980s, to which more recent institutional reincarnations such as Urban Regeneration Companies (URCs), Local Enterprise Partnerships (LEPs) and City Deals continue to bear some similar hallmarks, including neoliberal inflections, albeit variegated in their spatial compositions and manifestations (Pugalis & Townsend, 2013a). It could be argued that a series of policies designed to achieve quick 'wins' have predominated over longer-term strategic planning and spatially inclusive ideals, as many regeneration initiatives have sought to stimulate market conditions within fixed timescales. This reveals an underlying tension between more holistic targets that favour social objectives (seeking to serve local communities at large) and those seeking narrowly to organise and control space to maximise economic growth (primarily benefiting individuals and corporations through capital accumulation) that target areas of development and economic opportunity.

During the 1990s, the Conservative Government introduced the competitive 'challenge funding' approach, which included initiatives such as City Challenge and the Single Regeneration Budget. The popularity of competitive bidding regimes did wane to some extent under successive Labour Governments between 1997 and 2010. For example, flagship redistributive initiatives such as New Deal for Communities and the Neighbourhood Renewal Fund were based on quantitative measures of multiple deprivation that sought to targets areas of need. Competitive bidding remained prominent, however, as it became accepted among a growing neoliberal repertoire of regeneration tools. Hence, those in need of regeneration support have often had to compete with one another for the unofficial title of 'most needy', which has had the unintended consequence of generating a 'race to the bottom'. Alternatively, advocates, drawing in part on the Schumpeterian concept of 'creative destruction', contend that competition stimulates innovation and thus maximises outcomes. Regeneration outcomes under New Labour were at best 'mixed', according to Tim Williams, a former government advisor, who has since reflected:

> The evidence was mixed and many of these initiatives produced useful if isolated victories but it was clear that there was no great turnaround in the economic fortunes of the regions outside London and the southeast. All had benefited from national economic growth from the early 90s through to 2007 – largely founded we now know on funny money .... In certain neighbourhoods, often the ones we targeted for the New

> Deal for Communities poverty and deprivation clustered and indeed grew. Council estates, particularly those on the edge of the former industrial towns, grew to be bastions and indeed generators of social exclusion and concentrated poverty. 'Broken Britain', of which we hear even less now when it's getting more broken as an act of policy, was formed in such places at the moment Brown was grandiloquently announcing the end of boom and bust. (Williams, 2012)

Despite the considerable contradictions of New Labour's regeneration policy, which struggled to reconcile economic imperatives with social concerns, regeneration remained a key political priority, evidenced by the billions of pound of state expenditure. For example, the National Audit Office (2010) estimated that over a decade, the eight Regional Development Agencies (RDAs), excluding the London Development Agency, committed approximately £5 billion of state resources on projects with the specific intent of stimulating physical regeneration. Other estimates suggest that annual regeneration investment was as high as £4 billion per annum (GVA Grimley & PPS, 2010). It is in this respect that this period can be viewed as 'the golden years of regeneration' (Southern, 2013). With an economy still reeling from the effects of the 2007–08 credit crunch and a global economic downturn, it was apparent that the favoured (housing-led) model of regeneration predicated on the wide availability and easy access to relatively cheap credit to which the UK's public-, private- and third-sector interests had become accustomed was no longer financially viable (Parkinson, 2009). A change in the orientation and practice of state-led regeneration was thus apparent prior to the 2010 General Election, epitomised in the Treasury-led 2007 *Sub-National Review of Economic Development and Regeneration (SNR)* (HM Treasury, 2007). The election, however, provided a defining moment for the practice of regeneration and the significance of regeneration as a national urban policy concern. Upon accession to office, the Conservative–Liberal Democrat Coalition Government proposed what they claimed would be a radical 'new model' to rebalance the economy of England (Pugalis & Townsend, 2012). As a discourse and policy goal, 'regeneration' was sidelined by the interwoven narratives of 'localism' and 'economic growth', closely aligned with the Coalition's imperative to reduce the public budget deficit and to ease the reliance on public-sector employment. Although politics and discourses differ markedly around the world, many nation-states and especially those members of the European Union have accepted the necessity of fiscal austerity. Consequently, debate has been limited to the depth of cuts, the speed of implementation and the spatial distribution of such measures.

English regeneration programmes withered as funding was reduced by around two-thirds of the resources committed under previous spending rounds (House of Commons, 2011). There is a school of thought that states that even during the 'golden era' of state-led regeneration funding (during the first two terms of New Labour) the best that could be achieved was a sticking plaster to cover an open wound. Ashworth (2008, p. 21) states that 'pragmatic compromises' were often a central feature of urban regeneration as regeneration managers 'are often reduced to simply trying to do their best in the moment as they are bounced from one crisis to another'. The headline figure of a two-thirds reduction in funding arguably disguises deeper cuts to resources made available for holistic forms of regeneration, especially when one considers that new 'regeneration' resources include initiatives such as infrastructure enhancements, primarily focused on delivering economic growth that are essentially loans rather than grants (e.g. Growing Places Fund). Significantly, at the end of 2012, 'for the first time in over forty years there are no area based initiatives targeted at the most deprived parts of England' (The Work Foundation, 2012). It was as if state-led regeneration in England had been 'Con-Demned' (Pugalis, 2011) in a period when the rest of the UK was recasting their national approach to regeneration. The repercussions of a spatially unjust fiscal revanchism are potentially far reaching: for example, the 'extreme measures' taken by some US cities, such as the decision to permanently remove 1,300 street lights in Michigan (Peck, 2012).

This chapter analyses English regeneration policy during a climate of austerity. It explores the extent to which a transmutation in state-led regeneration policies has occurred, and analyses whether this is due to a pragmatic strategy to weather the economic storm or if it could indicate a more covert strategy to complete the right-wing ideological 'mission' fundamentally to reconstitute the role of the state, initiated by the Thatcher administration of the 1980s. Focusing on England as a window through which actually existing neoliberal repertoires can be examined may help to elucidate some broader trends associated with austerity politics and places under austerity rule. More modestly, the shifting contours of regeneration during an age of fiscal revanchism may serve to illustrate some of the repercussions when debates about the merits of regeneration are curtailed by a discourse that is only concerned with the depth and pace of cuts. The chapter helps to identify some of the primary challenges facing regeneration managers, and those with an interest in the governance and shaping of places more broadly, in a climate of austerity.

Methodology

The main body of empirical and secondary research that forms the basis of the analysis in this chapter was carried out between 2010 and 2012, and was subsequently updated in early 2013. The aim was to develop an understanding of the impact of the Coalition Government's urban policies and the emerging climate of austerity for the regeneration landscape in England. One of the key tasks was to compile a comprehensive desk-based literature review; this was completed by examining key contemporary and historical policy documents, relevant academic research and reports from think-tanks. To provide further depth, including qualitative information on what the era of austerity means for regeneration policy at the micro-level, semi-structured interviews were carried out with a number of regeneration and economic development practitioners (in the public, private and community sectors). The programme of interviews remains ongoing, as the research continues to track the shifting contours of state-led regeneration policy. Analysis is therefore provisional and explorative, with more detailed research reports and publications subject to follow. This chapter discusses some of the key issues that research participants highlighted within the new paradigm of austere public policy and its political antecedence, using selected examples from the interview data for illustration.

Structure

In the first substantive section, divergent interpretations of the practice of regeneration are analysed. The purpose is to understand the competing narratives and motivations that have guided the formulation and implementation of regeneration policy. By this means, the goal is to analyse the holistic conceptualisation of regeneration that integrates social, economic and environmental facets. This approach will be contrasted with a more economically focused approach to regeneration, which began to appear after the first decade of Labour rule (ca. 2007) and which has been intensified but also adapted by the Coalition Government. The conceptualisation provides the lens through which the policy shift from an integrated framework to a limited toolkit is examined. The following two sections identify the defining features and rationale of Labour's framework and the Coalition's toolkit respectively. By way of conclusion, the chapter identifies the marginalisation of holistic regeneration values in favour of economic growth objectives, and raises some challenges for regeneration managers.

STATE-LED REGENERATION: A BRIEF REVIEW OF CONCEPTUAL DEBATES

The concept of 'urban regeneration' is used here as a catch-all term to encompass terms, such as 'urban revitalisation', 'urban renewal', 'urban renaissance' and similar terms, as regeneration is a contested concept with no universally accepted definition. Different terms have found favour in specific countries at particular times and related to certain interventions. Urban regeneration is traditionally understood to be concerned with economic, environmental and social aspects, yet with a preoccupation with physical development activities that seek to redress social imbalances. Roberts (2000) refers to urban regeneration as 'a comprehensive and integrated vision and action which leads to the resolution of urban problems and which seeks to bring about a lasting improvement in the economic, physical, social and environmental condition of an area that has been subject to change'. Together with being a social, economic and environmental (physical) activity, regeneration is also a symbolic process that aims to foster a geography of hope. It carries an implicit message of resurrection, that 'something new' will be created, while simultaneously suggesting that a return to 'better times' is possible (Lovering, 2003). It is such regenerative properties that are distinct from other public policy pursuits, such as economic growth and development. The hope that is often conveyed in regeneration initiatives suggests that it may help to repair what has been ravaged by capitalist uneven development.

Urban regeneration is a form of place management predominantly concerned with the management of micro-spatial processes, but it could be argued that its neoliberal incarnation is preoccupied with the management of perceptions and products to help situate localities at the forefront of the global competition of cities (Lovering, 2003). Critiquing the middle-class gentrifying logics and consumerist tendencies of neoliberal regeneration efforts, Lovering (2003) observes that it 'is ubiquitously used to refer to a fairly standard set of policy goals and outcomes'. From this reading, regeneration responses, such as neoliberal repertoires, are emulated and mutated (to greater and lesser degrees) as part of the global–local mobilities of urban policy. This suggests that an examination of actually existing forms of practice in a particular jurisdiction may help to harvest lessons for other jurisdictions.

The identification of regeneration sites is not a spontaneous process: indeed, it is the opposite. Places are specifically chosen for targeted spatial intervention as a 'corrective' to the processes of uneven development. In this sense, state-led regeneration is part of an 'official strategy' (Lovering, 2003), rolled out to alter representations, practices and urban formations. It is a particular urban policy repertoire intended to temper some of the most visible and deleterious manifestations of capitalist uneven development, hence the designation of urban regeneration sites for special state assistance. Where social objectives remain important, this can result in channelling of regeneration resources towards deprived communities through, for example, specific area-based mechanisms such as New Deal for Communities. Alternatively, where economic objectives preside, this can result in channelling regeneration resources towards places of perceived growth potential, such as edge of city centre sites that were the favoured sites of intervention by the UDCs.

While many agents of regeneration consider that the central mission of regeneration is to improve the social climate, one tends, on cross-examination with project 'outputs', to find the striking dominance of 'hard' physical measures and outputs favoured over process (Pugalis, 2013). This paradox between stated strategic goals and 'final' delivery targets may explain why regeneration initiatives have long been criticised for failing to address deep-rooted structural issues. Trebeck (2007), for example, calls for a more nuanced understanding of transformations taking shape, which departs from the narrow range of socio-economic indicators by focusing on overall 'quality of life', which may help to challenge the tenets of regeneration. Attempting to negotiate between demand-side objectives, such as tax incentives, and supply-side objectives, such as safe living environments, is a persistent issue. Consequently, the debate continues about the effectiveness of area-based regeneration. Recent research provides some evidence to affirm that spatially targeting resources can reach concentrated pockets of poverty, but also cautions that the accuracy of targeting is non-uniform and, at a finer grain, found that the regeneration process bypasses many excluded people and households (Baker, Barrow, & Shiels, 2009).

In political–economic terms, state-led regeneration is administered to help repair the social, environmental and economic repercussions of capitalist uneven development. It is a capitalist policy instrument intended to respond to and assuage the outcomes produced by capitalist frameworks – a safety net of sorts. Conceptually, state-led forms of regeneration therefore remain locked into the structural logics of capitalism. In practical terms, state-led regeneration is administered for a variety of purposes, but can be distilled as a distinct form of assistance channelled towards particular communities of places. Assistance may include financial resources, political support, fiscal incentives and policy tools. Consequently, regeneration initiatives can perform as recovery strategies, which may be amplified in a climate of austerity, but can also be viewed as an unaffordable public expenditure (Pugalis & Liddle, 2013). The difference in ideological outlook partly derives from whether one views regeneration as a value-adding activity or whether one perceives it as an activity with a financial cost. These perspectives are not mutually exclusive and state regeneration investment decisions are highly complex undertakings. The key point to note is that regeneration is a political activity: the de-politicisation of regeneration should be treated with caution (Southern, 2013).

LABOUR'S REGENERATION FRAMEWORK

In broad terms, the Labour administrations from 1997 to 2010 pursued two key strands of regeneration policy: 'urban renaissance', which encompassed design-led physical regeneration and the reclamation of spaces of dereliction, with a city-centre focus, and 'neighbourhood renewal', specific area-based initiatives to tackle social exclusion. The Urban Task Force described the pressing need to create an urban renaissance, revitalising the urban core through high-quality design and the regeneration of brownfield sites, the review was heavily influenced by practice in European cities such as Barcelona and Berlin. Neighbourhood Renewal was a central feature of the first two terms of the Labour administration; it formed the social justice strand of the New Labour vision. The delivery mechanism was to be a plethora of area-based initiatives to enable 'problem spaces' to increase their economic activity and narrow the gap with more prosperous localities; the normative end goal, as Tony Blair famously stated, was that no one should be 'seriously disadvantaged by where they live' (Social Exclusion Unit, 2001). In theory, there was the potential for the two key regeneration strands to support each other and create a holistic framework for regeneration, but in reality there were also significant contradictions (Cochrane, 2007) and the potential for one agenda to undermine the other (see, e.g., the substantial body of literature on gentrification). Indeed, Turok argues that New Labour's strained urban regeneration policy displayed 'a tension between promoting economic prosperity and reducing social inequality. There are different ways this is expressed elsewhere: economic growth and social justice; competitiveness and cohesion; efficiency and equity; wealth creation and distribution; opportunity and need. Each means slightly different things, but they allude to a common challenge for social democracies' (Turok, 2008, p. 163).

The two major area-based policy initiatives pursued by Labour were the decade-long New Deal for Communities initiative (involving 39 deprived neighbourhoods) and the more widespread Neighbourhood Renewal initiative. Layer upon layer of area-based initiatives were introduced by New Labour, until the global economic conditions began to turn in 2007; the economic climate became toxic in September 2007 with the collapse of Northern Rock. The policy agenda then began to shift decisively from the holistic regeneration of place to the more modest aim to generate economic activity to bolster the flagging economy. However, the need for area-based regeneration initiatives and holistic regeneration had not radically changed; McGuinness, Greenhalgh, Davidson, Robinson, and Braidford (2012) report that housing and regeneration officers repeatedly cited the intractability of problems in many deprived communities; effective regeneration was hampered by the constraints of legal issues, construction delays and the need to achieve cooperation between partners. Interview respondents highlighted that a key restraint on progress was the need to 'match' funding streams, each with difference performance measures, outputs and timeframes, while ensuring community engagement and 'buy-in.' One regeneration professional stated, 'Residents don't understand the complexity of the situation – they think it's just a case of flattening the houses and building some new ones' (Stakeholder interview, 2010).

'Transforming places; changing lives: A framework for regeneration' (Communities and Local Government, 2008), issued by the Department of Communities and Local Government, was effectively a game changer and encapsulated many of the key messages and ideologies replete in the Treasury's SNR (HM Treasury, 2007), which emphasised the tensions between neoliberal and neocommunitarian objectives, namely increasing economic prosperity and reducing social inequality. The role of 'Transforming places' was to consult on a framework for confronting the root causes of deprivation in order to improve social justice by tackling the underlying economic challenges, which were perceived to be preventing places from reaching their potential. It aimed to

- tackle underlying economic challenges including worklessness by boosting enterprise;
- improve the coordination and prioritisation of regeneration investment;
- devolve power to more local levels so that programmes fit places through local and regional regeneration alignment.

This was a clear recognition of the deep-seated deficiencies of previous state-led regeneration policies that had failed to overcome structural issues. Yet, 'Transforming places' remained locked into the structural logics of capitalism. It did not at any level seek to challenge the causes of uneven development. As a precursor to an enduring politics of austerity, Labour's framework was intended to retain a safety net that would require less direct public assistance.

Self-styled as 'ambitious', much of the framework was fabricated from existing initiatives. At the time of its launch, it was also feared that the proposals were a 'done deal', which had prompted practitioners to focus on the more technical aspects of the package of proposals rather than consider the overarching objectives (Pugalis, 2008). The technocratic nature of state-led regeneration was a defining feature of the Labour years. Focusing on meeting targets, evidencing returns on public investment and demonstrating efficiency savings diverted attention from broader questions relating to the purpose of regeneration.

Extolling Third Way communitarian principles of helping people to help themselves by developing enterprising places to reduce worklessness, the framework laid out an agenda for improving the coordination and prioritisation of regeneration investment. Underpinning Labour's drive to achieve better value for money from regeneration investment was the principle that 'regeneration is a sub-set of economic development'. Prevalent here was the neoliberal orthodoxy that assumes areas of need and acute deprivation can be revitalised by spatially targeting investment in areas of opportunity.

As a means of extracting 'best value' from regeneration, Labour's technocratic method was to propose criteria to assess projects predicated on economic values, such as 'improving economic performance' and 'creating the conditions for business growth'. The technocracy was often burdensome and process-driven, which has been criticised for instituting a system that 'involve[d] a lot of targets and boxes to tick, lots of European, national and regional strategies, funding bids, business plans, accountancy for results etc.' (Bromley, 2008, p. 181). Driven by the intent to achieve better value for money from regeneration investment, the framework favoured an approach of enabling people to reach their full potential and preventing places from being held back economically, socially and environmentally. Referring to 'decades of de-industrialisation and economic restructuring' in the past tense indicated an extremely detached understanding of the economic challenges facing many urban and rural localities. The argument underpinning the framework was that direct investment in deprived neighbourhoods can often be very expensive compared with the economic uplift it generates, whereas reinforcing economic opportunities in central locations provides better value and greater success. Such economic tones were reminiscent of property-led regeneration initiatives launched in the 1980s that abided by a 'trickle-down' theory.

As part of Labour's top-down managerialist and paternalistic regeneration policy, they had a hyperactive tendency of experimenting with new structures of governance, partnership arrangements, performance management measures and special-purpose bodies. Each of these operated across different, albeit overlapping, governance scales and variously involved different, albeit overlapping, constellations of public, private and community actors. For example, cross-sector Local Strategic Partnerships were responsible to central government for delivering against targets established in Local Area Agreements (LAAs), while at the same time Multi Area Agreements (MAAs) between groups of local authorities and other partners were established, which again were predicated on the annual delivery of central government targets. As one interviewee expressed, 'Having been involved in previous MAA processes, MAAs felt very tangential to the real issues'. Such systems received criticism for devising technocratic institutional architecture and onerous reporting frameworks that transmuted regeneration delivery away from the realities of particular communities of places. Indeed, post-2007 Labour's scalar preference for neighbourhood-based area initiatives started to wane. This provided a key indication that part of the state-led regeneration safety net was being unravelled, although clothed in the rhetoric of enhanced coordination and greater prioritisation of regeneration resources – an economic investment. Communities Secretary, Hazel Blears, admitted as much at the launch of the Regeneration Framework, 'In an economic downturn, the public expects us to tighten up and target our efforts on people as well as places, which means employment and the economy'. Yet, it was perhaps the technocratic complexity of state-led regeneration that helped to mask the retreat from seeking to address social needs.

The framework suffered from some notable deficiencies. It lacked any consideration of how places of need can be more adeptly connected with places of opportunity, despite an escalation in area-based initiatives, partnerships and scales of governance over the preceding decade. Without a direct policy connection being made between places of need and opportunity, whereby connections would include a mixture of physical, social, cultural and economic relations, the Labour administration's recognition that some places 'have been slower to bring about a significant reduction in the number of people without work, and deprivation is still intense in some areas' was unlikely to find a suitable remedy. Hence, the state policy recognition of uneven development failed to comprehend, or at least acknowledge, that this is an outcome of capitalist modes of production, the result being that Labour's regeneration framework was not so much a holistic frame of reference for providing an adequate safety net for tempering the most destructive effects of neoliberal capitalism, but was more precisely a state-led attempt to transmute regeneration to facilitate the ceaseless quest for economic growth. Put in other words, regeneration remained locked into the structural logics of capitalism, and the safety net was being unravelled to help some people and places to prosper.

The economic climate had further deteriorated upon publication of 'Taking forward the regeneration framework' (Communities and Local Government, 2009). Consequently, the imperative of 'tackling worklessness', 'boosting enterprise' and supporting business during a recession was amplified, for example, with £418 million allocated to 20 Local Enterprise Growth Initiative partnerships between 2006 and 2011. By this stage, it was common for English regeneration managers to conceive of regeneration interventions as a means of delivering economic growth. Indeed, many considered that the primary role of regeneration was to promote prosperity, although this viewpoint remains more contested (especially among those operating at neighbourhood scales). In recognition of this prevalent regeneration mindset, the next section examines how the transmutation of regeneration has occurred since the Coalition entered office in May 2010.

THE COALITION'S REGENERATION TOOLKIT

Signalled in the pre-election political party manifestos, it quickly became apparent that with the installation of a Coalition Government Labour's technocratic approach, including their regeneration framework, did not fit with the Coalition's 'economic growth' and 'localism' crusade (Bentley & Pugalis, 2013). Indeed, it is noteworthy that the 'Local growth' White Paper rarely mentions 'regeneration', which is in stark contrast to the political attention that regeneration as a policy field received under Labour. The term 'regeneration', as is also the case with 'regions/regionalism' (Pugalis & Townsend, 2012, 2013b), has been largely omitted from the Coalition's vocabulary and, more importantly, this discursive absence has had a direct impact on regeneration programmes, as ministers have refrained from establishing any bespoke regeneration initiatives. If the state-led regeneration safety net was being unravelled by Labour, has this safety net been completely dispensed with by the Coalition? McGuinness et al. (2012) question the intellectual clarity and social equity of the Coalition's localist ideology stating the government appears to lack a coherent vision for deprived communities. The Big Society agenda is based on prosperous, well connected communities with high levels of social capital and there appears to be little allowance made for '... poorly connected communities where the confidence, connections and skills to solve your own problems are in very limited supply' (McGuinness et al., 2012, p. 262).

Arguably, it was a result of the House of Commons Communities and Local Government Committees' decision to launch an inquiry into regeneration that prompted the Coalition hastily to produce 'Regeneration to enable growth: What government is doing in support of community-led regeneration' (Communities and Local Government, 2011). This rudimentary toolkit is limited to a few pages of text and some appendices. Of central concern, the toolkit offered no definition of regeneration.[2] The Coalition has refused to define 'regeneration', claiming that 'it is not for Government to define what regeneration is, what it should look like or what measures should be used to drive it'. In contrast, the Scottish government published a comprehensive regeneration strategy at about the same time, which defines regeneration as 'the holistic process of reversing the economic, physical and social decline of places where market forces won't suffice' (Scottish Government, 2011), consistent with Roberts' definition of 'holistic' regeneration and similar to the notion of regeneration that guides Wales' 'New regeneration framework', which was published in March 2013 (Welsh Government, 2013). This affirms that the retreat from holistic notions of regeneration, consistent with a politics of austerity, is not necessarily a hegemonic trend. Indeed, England is distinct from other nations of the UK when it comes to conceptualising (or not) the goals and principles of state-led regeneration. As part of a House of Commons regeneration inquiry, the minister Grant Shapps was staunchly opposed to implementing a 'top-down national strategy for regeneration', suggesting that such a centralist imposition would impede a community-led approach (House of Commons, 2011).

Refusing to define regeneration and refraining from sanctioning any area-based regeneration initiatives of note were a clear signal of the Coalition's approach to fiscal purging: a localism gripped by financial cuts and devolving austerity. In the words of Williams, 'the sham that is 'localism' is their barely alive rabbit from a shoddy hat' (Williams, 2012, unpaginated). Indeed, denigrating the state as part of the problem would unleash further ‘incapacitation’, which Peck has observed across American cities (Peck, 2012). Neglecting regeneration practice and experience accumulated over several decades, the Coalition’s approach towards regeneration has been characterised as commencing from ‘year zero’ (Pugalis, Greenhalgh, McGuinness, Furness, & Errington, 2012). More accurately, they eviscerated Labour’s technocratic framework and prevalent regeneration practice of the 1990s and 2000s, which attempted to be holistic in its scope, design and intent. It is an attempt, according to Grant Shapps, to eradicate the ‘legacy of a draconian system of top-down targets that pitted communities against developers’. Yet, the Coalition also borrowed from and adapted the neoliberal repertoire of tools pioneered during the 1980s, such as incentive-based mechanisms, and there was also some continuation of policies pursued by Labour during the 2000s.

The outcome was that, for the first time in several decades, England was left bereft of a genuine regeneration strategy and accompanying dedicated resources. Under the guise of ‘localism’, the Coalition has, instead, provided a toolkit of instruments, from the New Homes Bonus to EZs, which are intended to dispense financial rewards for additional housing delivery and incentivise additional business investment respectively. More so, the toolkit is replete with incentives, tools and policies that convey a myopic mantra of ‘economic growth at any costs’. The sole focus on the economics of regeneration signifies a deepening of neoliberal regeneration policy encapsulated in Labour’s framework. Akin to Labour, the repercussions of uneven patterns of development, such as worklessness or deprivation, are considered by the Coalition to be a drag anchor on the quest for economic growth. To put it another way, the Coalition has completed Labour’s transmutation of regeneration from a state policy primarily administered to address societal challenges to one primarily administered to attend to market demands. Distinct from Labour’s approach, which perceived technocracy to be paramount to managing the regeneration problem, the Coalition perceive the ‘big state’ to be the foremost problem. Worryingly, the toolkit relies on many instruments launched in the 1980s that appear to rely implicitly on the much maligned ‘trickle down’ theory. It is unclear how localist community-led regeneration can be reconciled with top-down policies, such as EZs, and centrally administered resources, such as the Regional Growth Fund (RGF). Indeed, Lord Heseltine, the Chair of the RGF Independent Advisory Panel, was resolute that the £2.6 billion RGF ‘is not about regeneration’. A number of respondents commented on the manner that the RGF had centralised funding decisions for what limited public resources remained available, with one respondent stating:

> 'The RGF nationalised decision making – decisions are being made without the benefits of local knowledge. The process is flawed compared to the previous approach … [which] brought a lot of local strategic knowledge to the decision making process.'

Another respondent queried whether under the current depressed market conditions the private sector could step in and fill the void created by the extremely limited levels of state funding, observing:

> 'There has been an ideological shift with the government asking the private sector to take more of a role in the regeneration landscape. [However] … it is possible that the private sector is playing less of a role than it has in the past, due to difficulties relating to access to finance'.

Notwithstanding substantial criticisms of some of Labour's regeneration machinery, which a significant proportion of regeneration agents perceived to be 'very tangential to the real issues', in rendering such technocracy obsolete, the Coalition's toolkit had also dispensed with 'a lot of local strategic knowledge', often accumulated over many years of practice (Pugalis, 2010, 2011). The withering of regeneration as a public policy priority has been accompanied by a loss of skills, tacit knowledge and expertise. Views held by practitioners and councillors suggest that the present 'austerity-era regeneration' approach is a retrograde step:

> At the end of the day you only get regeneration outputs when money is spent, jobs are created or bricks are laid, for me it is about actual delivery and I can't see where the delivery mechanism is going to be.

The deficiency of mechanisms to aid regeneration helps to draw attention to spatial implications of a localism gripped by austerity. Despite claims that the Coalition's toolkit is designed to enable community-led regeneration, it has not gone unnoticed that risks and responsibilities have been devolved, but local autonomy over funding decisions has not followed suit. It is in this sense that Peck refers to 'an urbanization of neoliberal austerity', whereby it is something that central government does to local authorities, and local authorities do to deprived neighbourhoods (Peck, 2012). Austerity is devolved, but it can only be devolved so far. In the case of state-led regeneration, this is usually the neighbourhood scale, and thus it is those deprived neighbourhoods that suffer disproportionately. This analysis helps to unmask the spatial injustice that secretes the structural apparatus of the Coalition's neoliberal toolkit. Some researchers have warned of the dangers of 'cliff-edges' appearing between neighbouring areas (Turley & Wilson, 2012). Several interviewees indicated that the preference for economic opportunism (over socio-economic need) is likely to result in some longer-term spatial implications:

> Those communities where you have affluent, prosperous and well educated people are ready to take up the challenge. These are the places that don't need regeneration. The places that need it are the places that don't have … the aspirations, abilities, skills – they are the ones that will be left behind.

Although a scenario of some communities of places being 'left behind' was widely recognised by regeneration managers, and supported by evidence from the propensity of emergent Neighbourhood Plans to correspond with communities of places of 'prosperous and well educated people are ready to take up the challenge', there was a sense of resignation – particularly among local government practitioners – that there are no alternatives. It was as if the future path of regeneration had already been marked and a change in direction would not be possible. This was quite surprising, and can be contrasted with the rhetoric of localism that intends to offer enhanced freedoms, flexibilities and incentives that reward innovation.

There was a gut instinct among the majority of research participants that the Coalitions' approach was, at least in part, ideologically driven, a sense of an unfinished political agenda from the Thatcher era, although 'this latest austerity offensive is being prosecuted under historically and geographically distinctive conditions', that commences from an already neoliberalised configuration (Peck, 2012). Hall (2011) concurs, suggesting that, in the 1980s, only severe Inner City riots stopped the Thatcher administration carrying out a more extreme neoliberal agenda, by leaving 'the Northern regions and cities [to] face inevitable decline'. Such a policy theme was revived by the Policy Exchange in their 2008 report 'Cities unlimited' (Leunig & Swaffield, 2008; see also The Economist, 2013). Hall questions the future for the north, now that the Coalition has rapidly begun to remove the palliative of public-sector and quasi-public-sector jobs from the region:

> Is it simply proposed to cut off the codeine and the tranquilisers that have eased their long-drawn-out pain over the last three decades, leaving them on a minimal life support? Or is the real intention … to leave the North to wither and facilitate a great drift south? (Hall, 2011)

This fear, of a downscaled austerity politics, which actually exists in many American cities (Peck, 2012), was echoed by research participants, with one public-sector interviewee observing that '[r]egeneration doesn't feel like it has a place in [the Coalitions' approach] – regeneration steps in where things aren't working, but this government's attitude is, you just let the market take care of that'. In political–economic terms, the transmutation of state-led regeneration means that its administration to help repair the social, environmental and economic repercussions of capitalist uneven development is becoming more infrequent. The depth of austerity measures, involving the retreat of public-sector spending, reduced welfare support as part of a strategy to 'make work pay' and a focus on supporting 'real' jobs in the private sector, has proved challenging for many communities of places. This pernicious situation led one interviewee to argue:

> The UK governments' policy of 'don't worry lads, the public sector will contract and everyone will get a job in the private services sector', that just doesn't work outside London and the South East.

Indeed, those familiar with the growing socio-economic inequalities within and across London and the South-East (Dorling et al., 2007) would prompt a reaction that a regeneration safety net is warranted in all parts of England. The localism agenda, which, in the words of one research participant, challenges communities to 'sink or swim' is showing signs of reinforcing the competitive advantages enjoyed by more affluent places with economic potential and penalising those places traditionally the beneficiaries of additional state support (McGuinness et al., 2012). Conceptually, this may indicate that not only are current state-led forms of regeneration locked into the structural logics of capitalism, but they have been transmuted to support primarily capitalist growth. Equally, the Coalition's offer of greater autonomy to localities could be interpreted as a 'double edged sword', as one respondent stated: 'sometimes increased autonomy has come with reduced resources, sometimes it has felt like it has come down to us to make decisions where we cut investment rather than where we can make investment'.

From the situated perspective of this regeneration managers, 'localism' could be readily equated with 'cuts'. This raises new questions that concern whether greater autonomy has compensated for public-sector disinvestment. The Coalition's preference for a 'toolkit' over a 'framework' is perhaps instructive, as the former exudes connotations of self-help, where only the most basic tools are provided. Some research participants indicated that a depleted pool of state financial resources could result in more collaborative working arrangements, although the 'competitive tension', which the UK government is now endorsing, contradicts such an aspiration. Despite the toolkit's use of the phrase 'community-led regeneration', there appears to be a chasm, which continues to widen between such bottom-up initiatives and the top-down economic growth incentives (a chasm that was also all too apparent in Labour's framework).

The Coalition's approach to regeneration has been to treat it as a non-policy. In a report published by the Work Foundation, it was argued, 'Without regeneration, the most deprived communities in the UK will have little chance of economic recovery' (The Work Foundation., 2012). Interview responses corroborate this assessment and also extend it by suggesting that the loss of institutional capacity would have a disproportionate impact on peripheral regions: 'The loss of One North East will have a far greater impact than the loss of SEEDA for example. RDAs were at the forefront of things they were the "players" not the local authorities'. Conversely, a different interviewee highlighted the positive aspects of the process: 'taking the RDAs away and giving us a more direct relationship with the government … we are much closer to the people making policy, we have got a much better access around, opportunities like City Deals or Enterprise Zones'.

In a practical sense, there was a unanimous current of belief that replacing some of Labour's machinery, especially LAAs and MAAs, with more streamlined systems had improved central–local government relations. What the above interviewee extract also helps to identify is that a localist mindset is yet to penetrate the approach of all regeneration managers. The research participants held a strong presumption that central government is 'the [only] people making policy'. This also serves to support the perspective highlighted earlier 'that there are no alternatives'. With most research participants taking a pragmatic stance that 'as a society we cannot expect the same levels of service previous generations have enjoyed', it was also noted that the 'onus has moved to [communities] from government – "do it for yourself or don't have it"' localist brand of regeneration. One regeneration manager questioned the equity and practicality of this approach stating:

> it is what we were already doing, repackaged, with the onus on us, the government aren't going to do anything for you so you've got to do it yourself … it shouldn't be all about government hand outs, but sometimes it just needs that extra funding to get things in a position where they are sustainable … as it is, we are just going to be running to standstill.

In Peck's terminology, it reflects '[t]he neoliberal proclivity for downloading, by way of responsibility dumping and devolved discipline' (Peck, 2012). The implication is that, in some communities, there are particular cases where bottom-up forms of regeneration are thriving as they respond in creative ways to the shift from a grant funding regime to an incentives regime. Examples of community-operated post offices, public houses and village shops abound, together with the success stories associated with the transfer of 'assets' to voluntary-sector organisations. In practical terms, these are examples at a fine-grain scale of communities stepping in where the market (and state) will not – regeneration 'springboards' (Havers, 2013). The perverse feature of this trend, however, is that it is often, although not entirely, areas of opportunity that are benefitting from the regeneration toolkit devised for an age of austerity. In conceptual terms, communities equipped for the task (e.g. socially, culturally, professionally, financially) are able to provide their own safety nets and springboards.

While some interviewees suggested that deprived communities have been 'forgotten', an alternative perspective is that the Coalition Government (as well as other political factions such as Blue Labour and Red Tory) has represented deprived communities as an 'undeserving poor', signifying the end of more holistic forms of regeneration as we have come to know it (Southern, 2013). Respondents also remarked ruefully that 'it was not a great time to be in government [as a politician or officer], whatever your politics', with one interviewee elaborating on this sentiment by stating:

> There is an economic dimension but there is also a political dimension, in that the government has had to prioritise in terms of spending decisions … regeneration expenditure has been less protected than some other forms of expenditure; like the NHS [National Health Service] or adult social care.

It is such a sentiment that affirms the argument that the public policy field of regeneration has withered. Political choices have been made that have resulted in budget raids at national scales and left regeneration resources unprotected at local scales. To paraphrase Peck (2012), there has been a cumulative incapacitation of state-led regeneration.

CONCLUSION: CHALLENGES FACING REGENERATION MANAGERS

This chapter has demonstrated the withering of more holistic area-based regeneration policy ideals over recent years, specific to the geography of England and its unique historical conditions. This is in stark contrast to the perceived halcyon days of regeneration experienced from the mid-1990s through to the later part of the 2000s. Yet, a return to a regeneration paradigm of yesteryear is not being advocated. The issue at hand has been to draw attention to the transmutation of regeneration that has taken place, often concealed by de facto austerity measures and austerity politics.

Labour's regeneration framework attempted to outline how people, organisations and information could be marshalled more effectively to tackle deprivation and improve social justice by tackling the underlying economic challenges that are impeding places from prospering. It conceived regeneration as 'a sub-set of economic development', which was used to support a narrative that areas of acute deprivation could be 'lifted up' by targeting resources in areas of opportunity. Yet, numerous observers have noted that a 'rising tide' does not lift all boats by the same height (Cooper & Shaheen, 2008), and the results can leave some places 'sunk' in poverty. Despite such 'costs', the approach outlined in the Coalition's regeneration toolkit has intensified the competitive nature by which prospective projects bid for government support. In addition, the 'incentives' on offer are spatially selective, favouring only some social groups and some places. Substantiated by empirical material, this chapter has demonstrated how the incentives regime rarely favours deprived communities and has helped to unmask a spatially unjust neoliberal toolkit. The present policy preference is to target public resources in 'value-added' schemes that favour private-oriented objectives in a highly unbalanced way. This criticism can be traced back several decades, but has grown in prominence over more recent times. Indeed, it has been normalised by an austere state strategy, which has created a discursive space, which suggests that there are no alternatives. Most recently, 'regeneration' as a state-led policy objective and political concern has been virtually expunged from the Coalition lexicon.

'Regeneration' now appears to be at the mercy of capitalists seeking to maximise exchange values: a process contingent on market decrees of viability. In the words of one interviewee:

> Regeneration won't happen until economic development progresses and we see an upturn in economic activity, which will increase demand and that will start to fuel development, which will move into some major regeneration projects. Demand and finance are currently a depressant on the whole sector.

It is as if regeneration is no longer considered to be a role for the state. There is a perception held by some regeneration managers that regeneration needs to ride on the wave of economic growth. Hence, austerity politics has been accepted – largely without debate and resistance – as a convenient truth. Such views also affirm the broader point that state-led forms of regeneration remain locked into the structural logics of capitalism. But significantly, regeneration is no longer locked into repairing the destructive tendencies of capitalist uneven development, rather it is locked into assisting the quest for continued economic growth. This presents some primary challenges facing regeneration managers, which can be summarised as follows:

- *The changing role of the regeneration manager* – This involves a challenging remit of supporting community groups and other interested actors to regenerate places without necessarily having access to state grant funding.
- *The withering of regeneration as a public policy priority* – Without an official state definition of regeneration there is a risk that the objectives of regeneration will be captured by hegemonic interests. The policy priorities of the Coalition Government appear to have coalesced around a myopic focus on facilitating the economic growth of 'successful' places; managed decline appears to be the prescription for places that are not deemed to be competitive.
- *A depleted professional pool of regeneration managers* – The sector has had to contend with substantial redundancies over recent years as a direct consequence of the curtailment of state funding. Some regeneration managers were 'pensioned off', others have changed career and some are struggling to secure gainful employment in the sector. The result is a loss of skills, tacit knowledge and expertise.
- *The deficiency of mechanisms to aid regeneration* – For the first time in over 40 year there are no designated area-based sources of regeneration grant funding. The most deprived communities in the country are effectively having the life support system switched off. With the safety net removed, regeneration managers are looking to new sources of support, such as social enterprise.
- *The devolution of risks and responsibilities* – Austerity measures wield particular spatial manifestations. In terms of regeneration, the neighbourhood scale is particularly vulnerable, especially deprived communities that require a safety net. Throughout the New Labour era a level of bonding social capital was engendered in deprived communities, which is in danger of completely withering as community capacity building funding has been slashed and small-scale community organisations lose their fight to survive.
- *A neoliberal toolkit* – State crafted incentives are not necessarily strong enough to spur community-led regeneration. The limited Big Society branded policy tools that exist are designed for self-confident, middle-class communities which posses the skills, networks and experience to generate their own solution to social issues.

Collectively these challenges could lead to a sense of resignation besieging the mindset of overstretched regeneration managers. The debilitating view that all alternatives have been vanquished should be resisted. The retreat of the state reflecting a climate of austerity warrants consideration, debate and reflection. Such a reflexive strategy guided by the notion of a contested political economy is called for by Schofield:

> Instead of consensus on limited market failure impacting only on the most deprived communities – conveniently legitimising the next raft of 'regeneration' initiatives and lucrative, follow-on evaluations – we need a critique of market failure everywhere …. Political economy means just that, political choices for the economy. (Schofield, 2013)

While space does not permit the analysis of counter-regeneration strategies, views from the coalface indicated the complexity of locally derived regeneration practice and pointed towards some instances of progressive alternatives. Therefore, the apparent post-political consensus repositioning regeneration as a means to enable economic growth needs to be tempered with insights derived from practice on the ground – the actually existing forms of regeneration that often challenge and adapt state-led regeneration conceptions in novel and creative ways. Distinct from state-led regeneration initiatives that have been experimented with over several decades by political parties of different hues, actually existing forms of 'community-led' regeneration may offer some useful pointers to inform the design of future policy. Questioning the validity of subsuming regeneration to a neoliberal capitalist logic that 'the market knows best', the research indicates that the reverse may prove to be productive: understanding economic development as a subset of regeneration. Indeed, economic development is just one of several components collectively required to regenerate social spaces.

The curtailment of broader regeneration debates has framed discussions limited to the depth of cuts, the speed of implementation and the spatial distribution of such measures. The result is that regeneration, understood as a capitalist policy instrument intended to respond to and assuage the outcomes produced by capitalist frameworks, is no more. The safety net of sorts has largely been subsumed by a single-minded pursuit of economic growth, unless one is fortunate to reside in a community of place that is equipped for the task of community-led regeneration. Insights from regeneration managers suggest that these communities rarely align with the most deprived communities in most need of state-led regeneration assistance. A challenge for those wishing to pursue holistically framed patterns of regeneration in an era dominated by austerity politics must go well beyond technocratic and resource issues by restoring regeneration to a policy platform that demands a new political debate. The final word will be given to a regeneration manager who summarised the gulf between the reality 'on the ground' in deprived neighbourhoods and the Coalitions normative ethos of localism stating:

> ... in terms of volunteering [and doing it for yourselves] a lot of people just don't have the time because they are out their working. There is a naivety about how much can be done through this [localism] which frightens me.

NOTES

1. The focus of this research is on 'state-led regeneration', which can be defined as policies pursued by state actors that usually involve some manner of central government involvement (e.g. funder, policy architect). This is a much more restrictive definition of regeneration than is commonly applied in the relevant literature. Nevertheless, the definition of state-led regeneration is an important analytical distinction and has methodological implications.
2. The toolkit was updated in 2012, but continues to be exclusively framed by economic logics.

REFERENCES

Ashworth, C. (2008). Why do we never learn? *Journal of Urban Regeneration and Renewal, 2*(1), 19–26.

Baker, D., Barrow, S., & Shiels, C. (2009). How effective are area-based regeneration initiatives in targeting socially excluded individuals? *Journal of Urban Regeneration and Renewal, 2*(4), 351–363.

Bentley, G., & Pugalis, L. (2013). New directions in economic development: Localist policy discourses and the Localism Act. *Local Economy, 28*(3), 255–272.

Bromley, I. (2008). Reflections of a Torontonian in Sheffield. *Local Economy, 23*(2), 179–183.

Cochrane, A. (2007). *Understanding urban policy: A critical approach*. Oxford: Blackwell.

Communities and Local Government. (2008). *Transforming places; changing lives: A framework for regeneration*. London: The Stationery Office.

Communities and Local Government. (2009). *Transforming places; changing lives: Taking forward the regeneration framework*. London: The Stationery Office.

Communities and Local Government. (2011). *Regeneration to enable growth: What government is doing in support of community-led regeneration*. London: The Stationery Office.

Cooper, M., & Shaheen, F. (2008). Winning the battles but losing the war? Regeneration, renewal and the state of Britain's cities. *Journal of Urban Regeneration and Renewal, 2*(2), 146–151.

Dorling, D., Rigby, J., Wheeler, B., Ballas, D., Thomas, B., Fahmy, E., Gordon, D., & Lupton, R. (2007). *Poverty, wealth and place in Britain, 1968 to 2005*. York: Joseph Rowntree Foundation.

GVA Grimley & PPS. (2010). *Resuscitating urban regeneration: Surgery or supplements?*. London: GVA Grimley.

Hall, P. (2011). The economic geography of a return to Speenhamland. *Town & Country Planning*, *80*(7/8), 306, 307.

Havers, I. (2013). Small actions – big change: Delivering regeneration in the age of austerity. *Journal of Urban Regeneration & Renewal*, *6*(4), 426–431.

HM Treasury. (2007). *Review of sub-national economic development and regeneration*. London: HMSO.

House of Commons. (2011). *House of commons communities and local government committee, regeneration*. Sixth Report of Session 2010–12, The Stationery Office, London.

Leunig, T., & Swaffield, J. (2008). *Cities unlimited: Making urban regeneration work*. London: Policy Exchange.

Lovering, J. (2003). MNCs and wannabes: Inward investment, discourses of regional development, and the regional service class. In N. Phelps & P. Raines (Eds.), *The new competition for inward investment: Companies, institutions and territorial development* (pp. 39–60). Cheltenham: Edward Elgar.

McGuinness, D., Greenhalgh, P., Davidson, G., Robinson, F., & Braidford, P. (2012). Swimming against the tide: A study of a neighbourhood trying to rediscover its "reason for being" – the case of South Bank, Redcar and Cleveland. *Local Economy*, *27*(3), 251–264.

National Audit Office. (2010). *Regenerating the English regions: Regional Development Agencies' support to physical regeneration projects*. Report by the Comptroller and Auditor General HC 214 Session 2009–2010. National Audit Office, London.

Parkinson, M. (2009). Guest editorial: The credit crunch and regeneration. *Journal of Urban Regeneration and Renewal*, *3*(2), 115–119.

Peck, J. (2012). Austerity urbanism. *City*, *16*(6), 626–655.

Pugalis, L. (2008). A framework for regeneration: More questions than answers. *Journal of the Institution of Economic Development*, *106*, 7.

Pugalis, L. (2010). Looking back in order to move forward: The politics of evolving sub-national economic policy architecture. *Local Economy*, *25*(5–6), 397–405.

Pugalis, L. (2011). Regeneration 'Con-Demned'? *Town & Country Planning*, *80*(4), 188–191.

Pugalis, L. (2013). Hitting the target but missing the point: the case of area-based regeneration. *Community Development*, In Press.

Pugalis, L., Greenhalgh, P., McGuinness, D., Furness, H., & Errington, B. (2012). Chalk and cheese: A comparison of England and Scotland's emerging approaches to regeneration strategies. *Town & Country Planning*, *81*(2), 84–88.

Pugalis, L., & Liddle, J. (2013). Editorial: Austerity era regeneration – Conceptual issues and practical challenges, Part 1. *Journal of Urban Regeneration & Renewal*, *6*(4), 333–338.

Pugalis, L., & Townsend, A. R. (2012). Rebalancing England: Sub-national development (once again) at the crossroads. *Urban Research & Practice*, *5*(1), 159–176.

Pugalis, L., & Townsend, A. R. (2013a). Place-based economic strategy trends: England's fixation with 'fleet-of-foot' partnerships. *Local Economy*, *28*, 8.

Pugalis, L., & Townsend, A. R. (2013b). Rescaling of planning and its interface with economic development. *Planning Practice and Research*, *28*(1), 104–121.

Rae, A. (2011). Learning from the past? A review of approaches to spatial targeting in urban policy. *Planning Theory & Practice*, *12*(3), 331–348.

Roberts, P. (2000). The evolution, definition and purpose of urban regeneration. In P. Roberts & H. Sykes (Eds.), *Urban regeneration, a handbook* (pp. 9–36). London: Sage.

Schofield, S. (2013). The great regeneration swindle, *New Start*, March 12.

Scottish Government. (2011). *Achieving a sustainable future. Regeneration strategy*. Scottish Government, Edinburgh.

Social Exclusion Unit. (2001). *A new commitment to neighbourhood renewal*. London: Cabinet Office.

Southern, A. (2013). 'Regeneration' in a time of austerity will mean the death of this metaphor, but what will come next? *Journal of Urban Regeneration & Renewal*, *6*(4), 399–405.

The Economist. (2013). The urban ghosts: These days the worst urban decay is found not in big cities but in small ones. *The Economist*, 12 October.

The Work Foundation. (2012). *People or place? Urban policy in the age of austerity*. The Work Foundation, Lancaster.

Trebeck, K. (2007). *Looking at private sector contribution to regeneration: Problems, objectives, concepts and measurement*. Working Paper 7, Centre for Public Policy for Regions, University of Glasgow, Glasgow.

Turley, A., & Wilson, J. (2012). *Localism in London: The implications for planning and regeneration in the capital*. London: Future of London.

Turok, I. (2008). A new policy for Britain's cities: Choices, challenges, contradictions. *Local Economy*, *23*(2), 149–166.

Welsh Government. (2013). *Vibrant and viable places – a new regeneration framework*. Welsh Government, Cardiff.

Williams, T. (2012). People or place? Urban policy in the age of austerity: A response by someone with dirty hands. *Regen.net*, October 2.

PART TWO

CIVIL SOCIETY AND SOCIAL MOVEMENTS: CONSENSUS OR CRISIS?

In this section there are three essays which seek to reflect the dynamic and changing nature of the response from the streets to the economic and political crises from 2008 and beyond. In commissioning this series we wanted to encourage contributors to draw upon their insights and experience to inform their analysis. We wanted to encourage informed speculation and critical reflection. In each of these chapters we think that we have achieved that aim.

The different and, at times, contradictory nature of the resistance and opposition to the Age of Austerity can be seen in the discussion of the emerging social movements present in the Occupy Now initiative or the organised and campaigning projects co-ordinated by new and developing coalitions of community organisations. Or it can be seen on the streets of Cairo. We recognise that in inviting these contributions and facilitating these forms of critical analysis there will be moments when they read like dispatches from the frontline or that their conclusions are overtaken by events. We are not apologising for this. We think that each of these chapters (both separately and collectively) raise significant questions for those of us involved in public management and policy-making.

We can see the challenges that are raised for those who are managing urban centres or are working at a street or neighbourhood level to provide services across a broad spectrum from housing to education. The ownership, distribution, quality and values of these services are now under question in a profound way. On one level it is about the global crisis but on the streets of Cairo or Barcelona it is about the relationships between civil society and existing political, financial and business elites. In that sense it seems to us these chapters provide the lens through which we can observe the clash of values and ideas in a way which (perhaps) we have not seen for over 40 years.

THE STATE OF HIGHER EDUCATION AND TRAINING IN EGYPT POST THE ARAB SPRING☆

Dina Wafa

ABSTRACT

Purpose – *This chapter examines the ways in which the provision of training and development for leaders and managers in Cairo underwent profound change during the Arab Spring. It provides an important insight into the capacity of higher education institutes (HEIs) to respond to social and political movements and to the ways in which we might frame education and training.*

Design – *The chapter draws directly on the experience of the author and her colleagues as they responded to the explicit and implicit needs of*

☆An earlier version of this chapter was presented as a paper at the 2012 European Group for Public Administration (EGPA) Conference, Bergen, Norway, September 5–8, 2012.

Looking for Consensus?: Civil Society, Social Movements and Crises for Public Management
Critical Perspectives on International Public Sector Management, Volume 2, 89–104

ISSN: 2045-7944/doi:10.1108/S2045-7944(2013)0000002007

the social movements on the streets of Cairo during the Arab Spring of 2011.

Findings – *The chapter illustrates the extent to which HEIs can be responsive to expressed needs and it offers insights and understandings of the professional relationships between colleagues and participants as they seek to co-construct a new curriculum.*

Implications/originality – *The chapter examines important social change through the perspective of an HEI whose values are ones of promoting learning and professional development in a context where such ideas and concepts are being explicitly challenged and rewritten.*

Keywords: Learning; re-conceptualization; reflection; social movements

INTRODUCTION

Little did the 26-year-old Tunisian fruit vendor Mohamed Boauzizi know that when he set himself on fire on December 17, 2010 (Cornwell, 2011), in protest to an unresponsive government, the flames would soon spread to engulf the Arab region. Rage against dictatorship regimes sprung in a domino effect across the Arab region, from Tunisia to Egypt, Libya, Yemen, and Syria, while slightly touching other areas in the Arab world as well. During the process, four regimes were toppled. Today, two years later, the region is still in turbulence, each country at a different stage in its transition toward democracy.

Our focus of study is on the implications of the Arab Spring, and the transition period, on higher education and training in Egypt in general, with a focus on School of Global Affairs and Public Policy (GAPP) Executive Education unit at the American University in Cairo (AUC). The GAPP Executive Education unit is an income-generating unit serving government agencies and public institutions. The unit provides education and training opportunities that serve to reinforce and reinvigorate professional leadership capacities within government agencies, public institutions, civil society and media organizations in a challenging global environment within Egypt and the region. GAPP Executive Education offers both customized programs and open enrollment programs according to current trends and needs.

The Lead Up to the Uprising

In Egypt, the January 25 uprising in 2011 was driven by a need for change, citizen empowerment, a better quality of life, for freedom, and for human dignity. The principles of people power and participatory democracy were invoked in the Egyptians with their newfound sense of ownership and hopes for a better future. Egyptians were eager to participate in elections and referendums, after decades of passivity. They were eager for a better life and for embracing their newfound ownership and opportunity to be heard, and to have a voice, and they demanded their rights as citizens for a responsive government.

Though the 2011 uprising came as a surprise to many, yet the signs of unrest and dissatisfaction were clear. For several years, movements and protests were organized against corruption and government failure. The real surprise, though, was not that the Egyptians were dissatisfied, but that many believed that the dictatorship regime was immune, and had managed to suppress all signs of revolt (Darwish, 2012; Lynch, 2011). The January 25 uprising bore demands that united Egyptians from different religious, economic, and social classes. They found common ground, as they demanded a representative and responsive government, and for a rare moment forgot their differences.

Mubarak's regime was successful in increasing foreign investments and yet the economy failed to address the widening wealth distribution gap, the increasing corruption, and human rights violations. Various public sectors collapsed, including healthcare and education. Labor unions strikes were widespread due to economic deprivations (Bassiouni, 2012; Radsch, 2011). The most significant of which was the Mahalla district strike in 2008. Furthermore, several social movements such as "Kefaya" (Enough), "April 6," and "Kolona Khaled Saied (We are all Khaled Saied)" protested human rights violations and political grievances. "Kefaya movement opposed the inheritance plan of presidency and corruption, while the April 6 movement rose after the labor strikes in Mahalla district, and We are all Khaled Saied movement rose to oppose police brutality" (Kinninmont, 2012). However, these protests were considered isolated incidents that would bear no strong significance. Until finally, Egyptians managed to break the line of fear, and in 18 days toppled down a dictatorship regime. However, many today believe that the road to democracy is still a long one.

Prior to the January 25, 2011 uprising, in May 2010, the GAPP Executive Education unit was established. As the training arm of the school, its main focus is to provide training and learning opportunities for development to government agencies and schools. At that point, in 2010, the roadmap was clear, as is the case in any stable environment. The cabinet was stable, and so decision making, within limits, was available. The institutions' needs were quite identifiable, which facilitated the programs' planning process. Programs mainly relied on new pubic management models for improving efficiency, effectiveness and a service orientation. Applying theory to practice using a leadership-based approach in training and education methods.

Soon, Egypt was to find itself in turmoil of events. All operations were unexpectedly interrupted during the 18 days of the January 25 uprising. The government imposed a curfew on January 28, 2011, after cutting all Internet and mobile phone communications the day before (Bassiouni, 2012; Radsch, 2011). There was a communication blackout as all major Internet and mobile phone providers cut off their services. As Jim Cowie, Telecom expert and cofounder of Renesey's, coined it: it was as if the "whole country disappeared" (Channel 4 News, 2011).

GAPP Executive Education had to abruptly abort one of its long-term programs, the Advanced Public Policy Management in collaboration with the Ministry of State for Administrative Development (MSAD). Reaching trainees and trainers using the now rarely used landlines was quite a challenge. GAPP Executive Education, as with most institutions at the time, incurred due losses and faced uncertainty. The following transition period in Egypt and the region placed GAPP Executive Education at a test for responsive solutions.

One of the first challenges faced was location. Programs are usually run in the two American University campuses, one of which is located in New Cairo at the outskirts of Cairo, while the other is overlooking the famous Tahrir Square. The Tahrir campus is a preferred location by most participants for its proximity and centrality. However, this was soon to change. The million-man marches continued post the toppling of Mubarak's regime, continuously interrupted operations, particularly at the Tahrir campus. Safety was at stake, given that security forces had relatively withdrew from the scene.

The turbulent environment required extensive security measures to ensure the safety of participants, trainers, and staff, which resulted in additional costs to programs. Shifting schedules and changing venue became part of the usual operations and planning routine. During the past two years, Egypt witnessed numerous protests and demonstrations, mostly in the Tahrir area. Furthermore, some of these demonstrations escalated to serious clashes with security forces, resulting in serious injuries and blood shed, such as June 28, 2011, October 9, 2011, November 19–22, 2011, December 16, 2011, April 28–29, 2012, November 28, 2012, and the anniversaries of January 25. Naturally, programs would be rescheduled due to the turbulence, and yet again for other significant occasions, such as the parliamentary elections, presidential elections, or the two public referendums.

Post-January 25, 2011

During the past two years, Egypt witnessed two public referendums, one upper and lower house of parliament elections, and a presidential election. Participation of citizens was high. In Egypt, 49.2 million out of a population of 81.3 million (CAPMAS, 2001) were eligible for voting at the 2011 parliamentary elections (Elections Gate, 2011); for many, this was their first experience to participate for real in parliamentary elections. Voter turnout for parliamentary elections reached 54.99% in 2012, as opposed to 16.16% in 2010; and for presidential elections reached 49.62% in 2012 as opposed to 16.41% in 2005 (IDEA, 2013). Furthermore, the 8–10 million Egyptians living abroad, and whose remittances amounted to $7,725 million in 2011, were, for the first time, allowed to exercise their citizenship rights by participating in the voting process (El Baradei, Wafa, & Ghoneim, 2012).

President Mohamed Morsi came into power on June 30, 2012 after winning the elections with a 51.7 percent of the vote, and resigned his position in the Freedom and Justice Party (FJP) (World Bank, 2013). Following his appointment, Morsi passed the new constitution referendum. Endorsed by 64% of voters in a national referendum, Egypt's post-revolution constitution was passed in December 2012 (Amensty International, 2012; and World Bank, 2013). Historically, authoritarian regimes utilized constitutions, laws and elections to their advantage and to legitimize their rule (Owen, 2012). The new constitution and legislation were to set the road map for the future course. Yet, electing a president and drafting a new constitution were not sufficient to bring stability to a country that had witnessed a powerful uprising on January 25, 2011.

Currently, in Egypt, post the January 25 revolution, there is much debate and polarization among the different groups, whether secular or Islamist, on whether the past two years have led to increased government responsiveness as Egypt transitions toward democracy. Democracy challenges in developing nations are usually linked with the very basis of the prerequisite characteristics of active participation of citizens, protection of human rights, and a consensus of the basics of socioeconomic systems (Sarquis, 2012). In Egypt, though new political forces came into power for the first time, and the cabinet was changed three times, yet the country is still in turbulence. The anticipation for change and political ambiguity bears its implications on the economy and on public policy issues, and in turn on public management and public policy education and training.

Growth of the Demand for a New Discourse and Challenges in Delivery

Education institutes are expected to play a key role in economic, social, and political change and development. Initially, according to studies, their role may be only a responsive one, reactive "to external pressures rather than initiating or driving transformation" (Brennan, King, & Lebeau, 2004). In Egypt, education institutes have played a partnership role through facilitating debate and offering topics courses. However, the outcomes of the current struggle are expected to eventually lead to more pedagogical changes. People cannot be truly free without education to enable their effective participation in society.

The implications on public policy and public management education and training are inevitable as Egypt transitions toward democracy. These implications will naturally also bear significance on other specializations, as is the norm in interdisciplinary education, to include changes in media and journalism education, law and human rights, sociology, political science, economics, and history.

The general public had a thirst for knowledge and understanding. The GAPP opened up its Tahrir campus, in response to public demand, and offered the Tahrir dialogues. The Tahrir dialogues posed fundamental issues for discussion and analyses through a moderated panel debate of different viewpoints. Egyptian analysts and public figures were invited for debate amongst members of the media, civil society, academia, political parties, and the general public (Building a Better Egypt, 2011; Haroun M, Provost, AUC, 2011, personal communication to the American University in Cairo community). The dialogues were initially offered weekly and eventually biweekly, to date, and the halls were usually packed. There was a sense of ownership and eagerness to participate and learn amongst the youth.

Other schools were also quick to respond to the evident enthusiasm for knowledge through introducing new initiatives. Cairo University introduced new courses, such as the "Transformation of the Euro–Arab World

Relations Post the Arab Spring" (El Khawaga O director EuroMed Center, Faculty of Economics and Political Science, Cairo University, 2013, personal communication). The American University in Cairo also offered several topics courses including "Islam and Good Governance" offered by the public policy and administration department, "Revolutions in the Arab World" by the political science department, "Al Shaab Youreed Iskat El Nizam" (the people want to oust the regime) by the history department, and the Rhetoric English department offered "Writing the Revolution" (Building a Better Egypt, 2011; Haroun M, Provost, AUC, 2011, personal communication to the American University in Cairo community).

GAPP Executive Education responded to current trends and needs through offering the Free and Fair Elections program (GAPP Execed, 2010). Working in an environment where Egypt witnessed a referendum, upper and lower houses of parliament elections, and presidential elections in less than a year and a half required a quick shift of focus to Free and Fair Elections program. The focus of this program was on monitoring elections, the role of the media in elections, women empowerment, and political campaign management, and targeting media professionals, civil society, and political parties.

Education institutions were quick to respond to public demands for knowledge, yet they also suffered from structural impacts of the transition period. The turmoil of events posed several structural challenges including access, safety, funding, equity, and choice of language. The GAPP Executive Education Free and Fair elections program faced several structural challenges, of which equal opportunity and access were vital. Maintaining an education environment to enhance skills through debate and active participation in a classroom of participants from opposing parties required tactfulness. As an equal opportunity institution programs encouraged all participants without discrimination. When offering campaign management to political parties, GAPP Executive Education was keen to engage participants from all active political parties: Islamists, leftist socialists, center, and liberals all in one classroom. This posed a challenge, given the current polarization of the different groups, yet it was a challenge that had to be overcome for the overall benefit of the stakeholders.

Post the uprising, several newly formed political parties came to the political arena. Many were novel to the process of campaigning for a democratic elections. A balanced playfield would ensure one of the political objectives of the January 25 revolution, that is, democratic transition through free and fair elections. Yet most of the stakeholders were new to the process. Egyptians in general portrayed a passive attitude toward elections for more than 60 years. Programs such as the Free and Fair elections program geared toward acquiring skill sets in monitoring elections, advocacy, effective media, and campaign management represented an urgent need. One that is only the flexibility of training units may respond to. The target participants were mainly young media professionals, emerging leaders of civil society, and political parties.

Delivery of such programs presented an opportunity for training institutes to play an active role in Egypt's transition to democracy. Yet in addition to equal opportunity, other structural challenges were posed. One of which was the language of delivery. To maintain accessibility to the various stakeholders it was necessary to Arabize the curriculum. This represented another additional cost for translation of material and for depending on simultaneous interpretation when necessary as when sharing international experience. However, the added cost paid off through the increased reach out and inclusiveness of marginalized groups, breaking the barrier of language deficiency.

Several structural impacts on education and training programs posed an economic strain, including those of safety and of language. Yet the economic situation in Egypt post the January 25 uprising posed a far greater challenge. In February 2013, foreign reserves declined to $13.5 billion from $24 billion in September 2011 and $36 billion in 2010; and an expected budget deficit of 12.5% in June 2013 compared to 9.5% in 2011 and 8.1% in 2010. By October 2011, Standard & Poor's (S&P) downgraded Egypt's credit rating to BB-, due to political unrest, which was lowered further to C in March 2013; a sign according to Moody's indicating that there is only "a 10% chance of Egypt defaulting on its debt over the next year, and slightly less than a 40% chance of a default within five years" (Africa Research Bulletin, 2011a, 2011b; Reuters, 2013). By March 2012 the budget deficit in Egypt reflected a shortfall of GB 144 billion (Africa Research Bulletin, 2012a, 2012b). Furthermore, the Egyptian cabinet had changed three times, with prospects of yet further change. Identifying candidates was difficult with the constant change. Additionally, this resulted in a decline in the discretion of utilizing funds, as senior officials became reluctant to take financial decisions. This, in addition to budget cuts, led to a decline in investment in training and development. Usually, "training to support the individual career development of employees is more often embraced when budgets are flush" (El Baradei & Newcomer, 2008); budget cuts meant that the training line would be among the first to be affected. Prospects of further cuts are looming as Egypt faces an economic uncertainty.

Alternative means of funding were sought. Several funding agencies were eager to partner in change. Yet soon this was to pose a challenge. The Egyptian government released official statements through the minister of planning and international cooperation, and the supreme council of armed forces, who was in power at the time, denouncing foreign agencies and claiming that their funding was an interference with sovereignty (Ahram Online 2012; Feifer, 2011; Trofimov, 2011). This was further reinforced through detaining 43 foreign and Egyptian funding agencies staff and members of civil society organizations, and the spreading of conspiracy theory rumors in public (Ahram Online, 2012; Loveluck, 2012a). An action, which called for careful selection of partners and of ensuring a diverse portfolio of funding sources necessary to uphold programs and maintain credibility.

Prospects for the Future

Responsiveness to current trends is the natural outcome to external pressures. Will education and training institutes play a more proactive role to lead the transformation process? This is yet too early to assess. However, a glimpse on the history of changes in political powers in Egypt and its impact on education is far from encouraging. School curricula reflected a centralized government policy. The politicization of curriculum was utilized as a tool "to inculcate students with specific cultural values and understandings" (Loveluck, 2012a). The changes in leadership from Nasser's socialist era to Sadat's open market economy and to Mubarak's globalized capitalist outlook were clearly reflected on public schools' curricula (Baraka, 2008; Graham, 2004). Nasser introduced a free-for-all, centralized, public education system. An education system that simply encouraged memorization of text books, as opposed to free critical thinking and analysis. The socialist secular ideology was reinforced. Furthermore, Nasser's guaranteed public-sector employment resulted in a rapid increase in university graduates and eventually to a strain on public resources and productivity. This was followed by Sadat's open door policy, which created an opportunity for the spread of private schools; thus creating an opportunity for higher quality education, although memorization yet remained the basis of acquiring knowledge. Furthermore, Sadat introduced religion in schools curricula. Finally, Mubarak introduced globalization and diversity. Throughout, citizen participation was not encouraged.

Post the January 25 uprising, there have been no significant changes in public schools curricula, other than that the Ministry of Education removed all text referring to or praising Mubarak and the previous ruling National Democratic Party achievements, which comprised approximately 20% of the curricula (Loveluck, 2012a).

What will be the bearings of the rise of new political forces to power in Egypt on education? Elections brought a majority Islamist parliament, composed mainly from the Muslim Brotherhood Freedom and Justice party and the Salafist Al-Nour party. Furthermore, the elected president also came from the Freedom and Justice party. The rise of new political forces sets forth speculations on the future of education. Would Egypt follow the Pakistani model or the Turkish one? Pakistan has adopted a strict interpretation of Sharia laws in education, whereby Article 33 of Pakistan's 1973 constitution outlines education policy "to ensure the preservation, practice, and promotion of Islamic ideology and principles" and the National Education Policy sets Islamic studies as "the code of life incorporated in all education" (Nordic Recognition Information Centres, 2006). On the other hand, Turkey followed a more moderate example through increasing the number of Islamists officials in public office, and a few subtle educational reforms (Pupcenoks, 2012). Other controversies remain, such as allowing girls wearing veils into universities and the religious movements such as the Fethullah Gulen network calling for resuming imam hatip religious schooling for younger children. Nevertheless, the Islamist Justice and Development ruling party continues to portray a citizen's responsive outlook, downplaying confrontational religious issues. The shifting of forces in Egypt is yet to reveal where the road to democracy will lead.

Egypt's current ruling political party, the Freedom and Justice party, announced an encouraging higher education reform program. Reform outline includes advocating independence of universities, linking the curriculum with market demand, and increasing spending on research to 2.5% of GDP. Currently spending on research is as low as 0.2% of GDP, while higher education is 1% of GDP (Lindsey, 2012; Loveluck, 2012b). Egypt boasts more than 2.5 million students in higher education institutes. The higher majority are enrolled in public universities or public vocational colleges. Yet 18 state-run universities have a limited ability to generate and disseminate knowledge given their meager resources (Lindsey, 2012; Loveluck, 2012b). Currently a few significant improvements may be seen at the university level. Students are encouraged to engage in discussions and debates. Furthermore, student union free elections, a significant decrease in the appearance of police and intelligence services, and introducing elections for senior administrative positions as opposed to previous appointments (Lindsey, 2012) seem to indicate more freedom. Yet many remain skeptical. "In principle, one would hope that it would be easier to do policy research, but, depressingly, there seems to be no change. There seems to be a more active freedom of information movement, but it is not really making any noticeable progress. Revolutions need to invoke major transformations," stressed Emad Shahin, professor of public policy and administration (News@AUC, 2013). Furthermore, the second largest political influence, the ultraconservative Al Nour party, advocates linking the education curriculum to Islamic values and taking into account "the particular nature of women" (Lindsey, 2012), a stance that may negatively impact women's freedom and independence.

Faculty, continue to be skeptical, particularly regarding real change in policy issues. "There is general discontent when it comes to socioeconomic policies," said Ashraf El Sherif, assistant professor of political science (News@AUC, 2013). This is further intensified since the passing of the new constitution referendum. Endorsed by 64% of voters in a national referendum, Egypt's post revolution constitution was passed in December 2012 (Amensty International, 2012; and World Bank, 2013). Nevertheless, the new constitution, has led to heated debate and further polarization amongst Egyptians. Amr Hamzawy, professor of public policy and administration and former PM, claimed that the current regime's shortcomings are manifest in an undemocratic constitutional amendment process. Revolutions usually bring in their own constitution reflecting people's demands and ensuring proper representation for all. Yet the case in Egypt the case was quite different. A partnership to ensure transparency and inclusive of liberal groups and marginalized groups is essential for a smooth democratic transformation. Democracy challenges in developing nations are usually linked with the very basis of the prerequisite characteristics of active participation of citizens, protection of human rights, and a consensus of the basics of socioeconomic systems (Sarquis, 2012).

In Egypt the road map is yet unclear. Will there be a true transition to democracy or will Egypt follow the Sub-Saharan model where "restructuring did not occur, newly elected regimes often practiced old forms of repression or manipulated democratic formalities to their benefit" (Miller & Martini, 2012).

The ousted regime, though successful in increasing foreign investments and the economy, yet failed to address the widening wealth distribution gap. This, eventually lead to the January 25 uprising calling for bread and equity. Today two years since the uprising, Egyptians do not feel an improvement in their living conditions. The ruling party, the Freedom and Justice party, along with the second largest party, Al Noor party, seem to favor neoliberal policies, compatible with the previous regime. While the posed solution toward achieving social justice and equity demands seems to be through charity and goodwill initiatives (Kinninmont, 2012) for these two parties, such a stance is not shared by other opposition movements such as the leftist socialist movements and youth movements, who support achieving social justice through government policy and applying minimum and maximum wages to public office.

Economic policies will ultimately play an important factor in the success of the new political forces. The January 25 uprising calling for freedom, justice, and equity continues to have its repercussions in continued million-man marches throughout the cities of Egypt reflecting dissatisfaction. Currently Egypt has a population of 83 million and is expected to grow to 100 million by 2020; 70% of which live below the poverty line, more than 11.9% are unemployed, and 90% of the unemployed are youth (ILO & Ministry of Manpower & Migration, 2010; Radwan, 2012; Reske, 2011; World Bank, 2012). Currently there is a general sentiment of discontent as 86% feel that it's the government's responsibility, while 70% feel that the government was not successful in fulfilling social equity aspirations (Gallup, 2012). The failure to address economic aspects has led to much debate and anticipation for the future for a nation that demanded social equity, better government performance, and responsiveness. There is an urgent need to create a clear vision for the nation; one that encompasses employment and equity, the key factors leading to the popular unrest in Egypt. More important is linking education to employment, and market demand.

"Faculty members [at the American University in Cairo] anticipate that, rather than focusing on the productive sectors, economic policies will continue to emphasize free trade, retail, commercial goods, and brokerage" (News@AUC, 2013). A few inclinations and public officials statements are indicators for speculation and have lead to much controversy. El Morsi Hegazy, Minister of Finance claimed: "The new Islamic Bonds (Sukuk) law is expected to generate $10 billion for the Egyptian government" (Ahram Online, 2013). Studying the effect of the sukuk or Islamic bonds, and the reasons for its failure in Malaysia creates a ground for more informed debate. Additionally, there are no indications of increasing productive capacities as Egypt's revenue continues to depend on tourism, the Suez Canal, and workers' remittances, and foreign aid. Furthermore, the military holds a monopoly on major businesses, and is unlikely support any threat of greater competition with its own interests.

"Ultimately, the economy will have the final [and] is bound to bring about nationwide political change" (News@AUC, 2013). The impact of economic changes on politics and naturally on education as we have witnessed in the 2007 economic crises in Europe and North America is inevitable (Diamond & Liddle, 2012). Currently speculating alternatives and inspecting suggestions by the political forces are urgent to the course of economic development in Egypt. Alternative means and informed debate of overcoming the economic challenges are considered a priority need. Since "youth unemployment in extremis causes feelings of alienation from society and political processes, giving rise to social unrest" (LaGraffe, 2012), embarking on a national project to overcome unemployment and empower youth is one widely discussed option (Qassim, 2012). A project that would aim to resolve the mismatch between demand and supply in the labor market through creating effective labor market policies and programs need to raise youth employability and create more job opportunities (ILO & Ministry of Manpower & Migration, 2010). Egypt's large population of 80 million is composed of 54% under the age of 24, and 24 million between the ages of 15 and 29, "also referred to in the demographic security field as 'fighting age'" (LaGraffe, 2012). The challenge is to turn this resource into a productive one. During and immediately after the uprising, youth volunteered to help protect their districts in the absence of security forces, and they organized task forces to help clean the streets, organize traffic, and to provide medical and food supplies. The outbursts of volunteerism is a clear sign of the high potential resource in deploying this energy for development.

CONCLUSION

Education and training institutions have a potential vital role to play in partnering in Egypt's transition to democracy. The initial response to the impact of the economic, social, and political changes on executive education training, and on public administration and research in Egypt is a reactionary responsiveness. This is natural. Yet a more proactive driving force toward transformation is needed in the coming phase of transition. Education institutes are expected to play a key role in economic, social, and political change and development.

The initial impact is mainly structural: access, safety, funding, equity, and choice of language. Responsiveness and flexibility toward addressing these issues is essential. The quick and more significant change can be seen more clearly in the training and executive education, which offer more flexibility and responsiveness. The costs may be high initially. However, the outcome is the primary focus in a transition period. The bases of development curricula are already in place; the debate is on when, and if, policy issue changes do occur and how they will bear significance on education.

During the two years following the January 25 uprising, there has been social unrest, as challenges between the newly emergent political forces of power have not yet stabilized. The economy is deteriorating and inequity continues. These are essential factors that need to be addressed as a basis for development. Harnessing the newfound outbursts of ownership, sense of pride and belonging, which were thought to have perished among the long years of corruption and dictatorship, is necessary to providing creative solutions to emerge from the crises. Youth empowerment and matching education and training with market needs are a prerequisite for stability and security. People cannot be truly free without education to enable their effective participation in society Empowering citizens to create a balance in power toward a responsive accountable government.

REFERENCES

Africa Research Bulletin. (2011a). All three indices show a return of confidence. *Africa Research Bulletin*, *48*(7), 19202.

Africa Research Bulletin. (2011b). Fragile transition. *Africa Research Bulletin*, *48*(10), 19297–19298.

Africa Research Bulletin. (2012a). Transition plans. *Africa Research Bulletin*, *49*(2), 19191.

Africa Research Bulletin. (2012b). Filling the deficit. *Africa Research Bulletin*, *49*(3), 19489.

Ahram Online. (2012). *Egypt parliament to consider rejecting US aid*. Retrieved from http://english.ahram.org.eg/NewsContent/3/12/36526/Business/Economy/Egypt-parliament-to-consider-rejecting-US-aid.aspx. Accessed on July 2, 2012.

Ahram Online. (2013). *Islamic bonds to generate $10 billion in revenue: Egypt FM*. Retrieved from http://english.ahram.org.eg/NewsContent/3/12/62910/Business/Economy/Islamic-bonds-to-generate–billion-in-revenue-Egyp.aspx. Accessed on March 21, 2013.

Amnesty International. (2012). Egypt's New Constitution Limits Fundamental Freedoms and Ignores the Rights of Women. Retrieved from http://www.amnesty.org/en/news/egypt-s-new-constitution-limits-fundamental-freedoms-and-ignores-the-rights-of-women. Accessed on 17 January 2013.

Baraka, P. E. (2008). Citizenship education in Egyptian public schools: What values to teach and in which administrative and political contexts? *Journal of Education for International Development*, *3*(3), 1–18. Retrieved from http://www.equip123.net/jeid/articles/7/Baraka-CitizenshipEducation.pdf. Accessed on November 28, 2012.

Bassiouni, A. (2012). *Egypt's Revolution*. Cairo: National Association for Culture.

Brennan J., King, R., & Lebeau, Y. (2004). *The role of universities in the transformation of societies: An international research project. Center for Higher Education Research & Information and Association of Commonwealth Universities, London*. Retrieved from http://www.open.ac.uk/cheri/documents/transf-final-report.pdf. Accessed on March 21, 2013.

Building a Better Egypt. (2011). Retrieved from http://www.aucegypt.edu/GAPP/Pages/BuildingaBetterEgypt.aspx. Accessed on July 12, 2012.

CAPMAS. Central Agency for Public Mobilization and Statistics. (2001). "The permanent migration of Egyptians 2000". As quoted in: International Organization for Migration (IOM) (2010). A Study on the Dynamics of the Egyptian Diaspora: Strengthening Development Linkages. Cairo: IOM.

Channel 4 News. (2011). *Egypt in virtual communications blackout*. Retrieved from http://www.channel4.com/news/egypt-in-virtual-communications-blackout Accessed on May 17, 2013.

Cornwell, R. (2011). Ten people who changed the world: Mohammed Bouazizi, an ordinary man who became the Arab Spring's figurehead. *The Independent*. Retrieved from http://www.independent.co.uk/news/world/politics/ten-people-who-changed-the-world-mohammed-bouazizi-an-ordinary-man-who-became-the-arab-springs-figurehead-6282311.html Accessed on May 11, 2013.

Darwish, N. (2012). *The Devil We Don't Know*. New York, NY: Wiley-Blackwell.

Diamond, J., & Liddle, J. (2012). Reflections and speculations on teaching and learning in public administration. *Public Policy and Administration*, *27*(3), 265–277.

El Baradei, L., & Newcomer, K. (2008). A human capital management assessment tool for identifying training and development needs: Application to Egyptian public organisations. *International Journal Public Sector Performance Management*, *1*(2), 119–149.

El Baradei, L., Wafa, D., & Ghoneim, N. (2012). Assessing the voting experience of egyptians abroad: Post the 25 January revolution. *Journal of US-China Public Administration*, *9*(11), 1223–1243.

Elections Egypt Web site. Retrieved from http://www.elections2011.eg/ Accessed on 30 December 2011.

Feifer, G. (2011). Looking for opportunity in the Egyptian crises. *Radio Free Europe*. Retrieved from http://www.rferl.org/content/egypt_united_states_commentary_mubarak_obama/2296838.html. Accessed on July 1, 2012.

Gallup. (2012). *MENA residents put onus on government to help the poor*. Retrieved from http://www.gallup.com/poll/158906/mena-residents-put-onus-government-help-poor.aspx Accessed on December 20, 2012.

GAPP Execed. (2010). Retrieved from http://www.aucegypt.edu/GAPP/execed/Pages/default.aspx. Accessed on July 12, 2012.

Graham, E. (2004). *Islamic extremism & modern Egypt*. Retrieved from http://www.mideast-info.com/archive/paper4.htm. Accessed on March 21, 2013.

Haroun, M. AUC Provost. (2011). An Educational Initiative in the Spirit of New Egypt Personal Communication to the AUC Community, 24 February 2011.

IDEA. (2013). *Voter turnout data for Egypt*. Retrieved from http://www.idea.int/vt/country-view.cfm?CountryCode=EG. Accessed on May 12, 2013.

ILO and Ministry of Manpower and Migration. (2010). *Youth employment national action plan 2010–2015*. Retrieved from http://www.ilo.org/public/english/region/afpro/cairo/downloads/nap_e.pdf. Accessed on July 15, 2012.

Kinninmont, J. (2012). *Bread, dignity and social justice: The political economy of Egypt's transition*. Retrieved from http://www.chathamhouse.org/publications/papers/view/183047. Accessed on November 15, 2012.

LaGraffe, D. (2012). The youth bulge in Egypt: An intersection of demographics, security, and the Arab spring. *Journal of Strategic Security*, *5*(2), 65–80.

Lindsey, U. (2012) Freedom and reform at Egypt's universities. *Carnegie Endowment for International Peace*. Retrieved from http://carnegieendowment.org/2012/09/04/freedom-and-reform-at-egypt-s-universities/drak. Accessed on March 21, 2013.

Loveluck, L. (2012a). *The contradictory aims of USAID in Egypt*. Retrieved from http://www.opendemocracy.net/louisa-loveluck/contradictory-aims-of-usaid-in-egypt Accessed on July 2, 2012.

Loveluck, L. (2012b). *Education in Egypt: Key challenges*. Chatham House. Retrieved from http://www.chathamhouse.org/publications/papers/view/182603. Accessed on 21, March 2013.

Lynch, M. (2011). *The Arab Uprising: Unfinished Revolution of the new Middle East*. New York, NY: Public Affairs.

Miller L. & Martini J. (2012). How does Arab Spring compare to third wave transitions? Retrieved from http://www.rand.org/blog/2012/08/how-does-arab-spring-compare-to-third-wave-transitions.html. Accessed on January 31, 2013.

News@AUC. (2013). Faculty reflect on second anniversary of January 25, future prospects. Retrieved from http://www.aucegypt.edu/newsatauc/Pages/story.aspx?eid = 1024&utm_sourcenewsatauc. Accessed on January 27, 2013.

Nordic Recognition Information Centres. (2006). Report on the system of education in Pakistan. Retrieved from http://www.nokut.no/Documents/NOKUT/Artikkelbibliotek/Kunnskapsbasen/Konferanser/SU%20konferanser/Seminarer/Fagseminar_06/The%20System%20of%20Education%20in%20Pakistan.pdf. Accessed on March 21, 2013.

Owen, R. (2012). *The rise and fall of Arab presidents for life*. Cambridge: Harvard University Press.

Pupcenoks, J. (2012). Democratizatic Islamization in Pakistan and Turkey: Lessons for the post-Arab spring Muslim world. *Middle East Journal*, *66*(2), 273–294.

Qassim, H. (2012). *Bernamig al-Murashah [The Candidate's Program]*. Cairo: Dar El Nasr.

Radsch, C. C. (2011). *Blogosphere and social media In Laipson E Seismic shift: Understanding Change in the Middle East* (pp. 67–82). Washington, DC: Henry L. Stimson Center.

Radwan, S (2012). *The Egyptian economy: Waiting for a miracle?* Retrieved from http://carnegie-mec.org/publications/?fa = 49929. Accessed on December 20, 2012.

Reske, H. (2011). *Egypt's poverty, unemployment push youths to breaking point*. Available at http://www.newsmax.com/Newsfront/Egypt-poverty-unemployment-unrest/2011/01/31/id/384555. Accessed on July 15, 2012.

Reuters. (2013). *Moody's downgrades Egypt's credit rating*. Retrieved from http://www.voanews.com/content/moodys_downgrades_egypt_citing_unsettled_political_conditions_weak_finances_reuters/1626276.html. Accessed on March 23, 2013.

Sarquis, D. (2012). Democratization after the Arab Spring: The case of Egypt's political transition. *Politics & Policy*, *40*(5), 871–903.

Trofimov, Y. (2011). Egypt opposes U.S.'s democracy funding. *The Wall Street Journal*. Retrieved from http://online.wsj.com/article/SB10001424052702304665904576383123301579668.html. Accessed on December 20, 2012.

World Bank. (2012). *Egypt overview*. Retrieved from http://www.worldbank.org/en/country/egypt/overview. Accessed on December 20, 2012.

World Bank. (2013). Egypt Overview. Retrieved from http://www.worldbank.org/en/country/egypt/overview.print. Accessed on16 April 2013.

RESIST, REFUSE, OCCUPY

Graeme Chesters

ABSTRACT

Purpose – *This chapter examines the potential significance of the 'Occupy' movement across Europe and North America. It argues that an understanding of the movement is necessary in order to locate its significance (or not) in the broader reaction to the banking collapse.*

Design – *The chapter draws on the literature and is intentionally speculative in its approach.*

Findings – *The chapter argues that the Occupy movement is one manifestation of the alter-globalisation movement. This movement has been explicitly opposed to neoliberal ideas. This chapter suggests that the current crisis represents a much more systematic challenge for global capitalism.*

Implications /originality – *This chapter represents an original and important contribution to our understanding of the conceptual and theoretical ideas present amongst those resisting the impacts of the financial crisis.*

Keywords: Disaster capitalism; neoliberal; occupy; social movements

Looking for Consensus?: Civil Society, Social Movements and Crises for Public Management
Critical Perspectives on International Public Sector Management, Volume 2, 105–121

ISSN: 2045-7944/doi:10.1108/S2045-7944(2013)0000002008

INTRODUCTION

This chapter addresses the significance of the Occupy movement for those attempting to understand institutional and civil society responses to the financial 'crisis'. It argues that this movement and the events it is seen to be a reaction against are significant in that they reveal something of the convergence of crises (ecological, institutional, financial and democratic) that form the context and backdrop for all contemporary social and political action. The chapter embraces the call by the editors 'to take an idea for a walk,' so rather than describing in detail the empirical travails of Occupy as a movement, it tries instead to set out the 'stakes' that are being revealed by its actions and to assess the direction of travel the movement suggests.

The author argues that Occupy is the latest manifestation of what is variously known as the alter globalisation movement (AGM) or global justice movement, which has systematically and explicitly contested the spread of neoliberal capitalism and the forms of governance associated with it, both political and financial, over a 20-year period (Chesters & Welsh, 2006). It will argue that the critique of neoliberalism developed by this movement has been dramatised through the institutional and political crises now being experienced in the 'advanced' and informationalised democracies associated with the spread of neoliberalism. It will further suggest that the approach of accelerating business as usual, or what Naomi Klein (2007) describes as 'disaster capitalism', is both destructive and simultaneously indicative of the present limits to institutional politics. These are the same limits that are widely recognised and discussed by political elites (Rodrik, 2011; Stiglitz, 2007) despite their notable absence within everyday political discourse.

The chapter begins by sketching out a little of the background and context of global neoliberalism and the fracture lines it has induced, as well as the dynamics it set in motion and the subsequent impacts these have had for political, economic and social life. It then moves on to outline the basis for contemporary anti-capitalism and to differentiate between contemporary anti-capitalist movements such as Occupy and previous anti-capitalist movements that were concerned with state capture and command economics. Finally, it describes the praxis of Occupy as asserting the idea of the commons against both the newly privatised enclosures of corporate life, and the 'public spaces' that are opened and closed by the state. It also argues that in the practice and popularity of Occupy we can observe an otherwise repressed desire for democratic participation and the public unfolding of a new utopianism in politics, stemming from a need for creative solutions to the convergence of crises that are exacerbated by neoliberal ideology.

NEOLIBERALISM AS NORM – THE EFFECTS OF ECONOMIC GLOBALISATION

> That capitalism naturalizes its market model of the economy is understandable; the idea of a world organized in terms of individuals, self-regulating markets, and commodities is necessary to the functioning of the system. Less understandable is a certain naturalization of capital as the central organizing principle of social life in the critical discourses of political economy. (Escobar, 2008, p. 74).

Much as been written about neoliberalism (Davis & Monk, 2009; Harvey, 2007; Stedman-Jones, 2012) and its 'crisis', 'fall', 'death' or even 'strange non-death' (Crouch, 2013). Suffice to say, that in this context I am presuming a familiarity with the major contours of neoliberal ideology – the elevation of market mechanisms, privatisation and deregulation of crucial economic and social goods, the privileging of monetary policy and the minimisation of government interference in the 'market-place'. Instead of casting a backward glance towards the founders and intellectual and political champions of this ideology, I want to try to trace some of the outcomes and effects it has had upon social and political life and the way it has become codified as the norm. This ideology has, after all, provided the contours for an experiment that we have been living for some 30 years or more.

Contemporary neoliberalism re-emphasises the individual in the context of a global process of economic deregulation that extends government through 'governance' so that market mechanisms, messages and signals become means of control, orchestrating day-to-day life. This involves re-regulation – to support the privatisation and marketisation of the public sector – and re-responsibilisation – the remaking of citizens as customers and consumers (Larsson, Letell, & Thorn, 2012). Whether this is through performance management or institutional league tables, target setting or consumer preference, life becomes oriented towards the 'business' of living rather than the goals of a good life. Further, neoliberalism promotes this business globally through supposedly 'democratic' institutions responsible for trade agreements, loans and economic regulation in regimes that codify this system of rules. Although citizens usually have no direct role in electing members of these institutions, they function as a key part of the 'high politics' of democracy – a politics that in the view of many social movements is profoundly anti-democratic. Direct violence is added to this contemporary system of rules by adopting the strategy of pre-emptive use of military force against *perceived* threats to democracy. Combined with programmes of state building and the assertion of inviolable basic values, this system then represents a claim to primacy as the benchmark for human civilisation.

The embedding of neoliberalism at an international level has been enabled through the 'global regulatory reach' (Welsh, 2000) of economic and financial regulatory regimes, such as those of the World Bank and IMF, some of which are tied to technical aid programmes and/or facilitated by military intervention. Whilst such regimes typically leave some leeway in terms of how they are implemented to accommodate cultural differences, they are primarily shaped by Western forms of rationality through expert communities. Global regulatory reach assumes that the substantive rationality underpinning a particular economic or 'development' programme can be realised irrespective of the cultural and social composition and traditions of recipient states. Further, there is an implicit assumption that the citizens of recipient states will accept the discipline and outcomes of such regimes and the necessary lifestyle adjustments they require. The increasing attention given to 'governance' issues and 'civil society questions' in the IMF and World Bank thus, in part, reflects the increasing resistance of actors in both South and North to such exercises in global regulatory reach.

In this process, states become increasingly torn between competing externalities as they attempt to simultaneously align themselves with the smoothing and striating forces of capital, science, technology and citizen demands The notion of states as guarantors of national capital(s) – the executive committee model of the state – becomes decisively fractured. The modern state is increasingly fragmented as different departments of state align themselves differentially in relation to the range of external and internal pressures. The classic functions of the state interact with the global institutional nexus and the 'security state', 'finance state' and 'political state' constitute and become subject to top-down regimes (Chesters & Welsh, 2006). These lines of fracture are reflected within the global institutional nexus as part of the struggle to assert the primacy of neoliberal global agendas. Some have described this nexus as an integrated *Empire* (Hardt & Negri, 2000); however, this results in an over hegemonic depiction of the prevailing power relations. There are in effect competing *Empires* as different *fractions* align in the pursuit of competing agendas. The interpretation of these fault lines and the alignment of 'domestic policy' within particular nation states thereby produces increasing fragmentation of the 'national'.

In much of the 'West', the generalisation of this state–corporate enterprise has extended to public institutions such as schools, hospitals, universities and prisons transforming and diminishing the 'public sphere'. The spread of shopping malls as private developments restricts rights of assembly within urban centres[1] and persistent protests against controversial corporate activities result in the definition of legitimate 'protest zones', which are often distant from the actual sites. This is further enforced by state surveillance agencies increasingly targeting citizens in a wide range of social movement activities, sometimes spending public resources to fund long-term undercover penetration of these movements without any visible operational gains (Hattenstone, 2011). The enactment of opposition in these concrete sites results in myriad instances where the *symbolic stakes* of state–corporate activity coordinated through a global institutional nexus are contested, exposing more and more citizens to the increasing array of carefully targeted laws which seek to discipline and punish.

This is particularly pronounced in sectors perceived as central to future economic prosperity. In the 1970s, 'anti-nuclear' movements were denounced as dupes of the Soviet Union, amidst claims that they were recipients of 'Russian gold', aimed at denying the 'West' the benefits of nuclear energy. From the 1980s onwards, environmental protestors, climate change activists and social justice campaigners, along with a range of other groups, have been targeted as enemies within in an era dominated by the fear of network actors – a fear rendered material by the events of 9/11.

THE STRUCTURAL VIOLENCE OF NEOLIBERALISM

This discursive targeting of those resisting neoliberal orthodoxy now occurs in a very different context compared to the 'late corporatism' of the 1970s. The neoliberal market message 'maximise shareholder value' is apparently decoupled from the dual identity of shareholders – whether as direct investors or contributors to pension funds or as citizen/subjects confronted by multiple and frequently contradictory demands. The better value a stock is of, the more ruthless its corporate culture must be in the entrepreneurial pursuit of innovation. The investor citizen may prosper in terms of dividend rates but must live with the consequences of the increasingly pathological divisions of labour required by deregulated, flexible labour markets, something that is reflected by shifts in the structure of language to incorporate these changes – such as when *Karioshi* or death from overwork entered the Japanese language (McCormack, 1991).

Corporate executives held responsible for misappropriation of pension funds, fraudulent liquidity statements, misrepresentation of research on product health impacts and so on leave with enhanced severance packages. Corporate employees meanwhile work on insecure short-term contracts in flexible labour markets – an intensely competitive and insecure environment where the right to hire and fire is foregrounded within a climate of corporate governance that notionally aspires to encourage employee cooperation and participation. Within this 'mad house' of 'casino capitalism' (Hutton, 2002) talent migrates rapidly to the highest bidder, labour market turnover increases and ever more elaborate job titles and descriptions are conjured up to make people feel valued. Short-term contracts and comparatively modest salaries promote work nomadism to countries with better remuneration as individuals with the relevant transferable skills seek to maximise their life chances outside the container of the nation state. The relocation of sectors of the economy, such as the biotechnology industry to developing nations, in turn inverts the flow of ethnically constituted labour associated with Fordism and post-Fordism by taking the techniques to the subjects.

This is the logic of globalisation and deregulation – it is something that was advanced and negotiated within the architecture of global high politics including the G8, IMF, World Bank and WTO. Where it was asserted that 'globalisation is the only game in town' – our political and economic leaders laid the foundations for it, they are the notional ringmasters, they *would* say that – their political parties are largely reliant upon corporate sponsorship – meaning they *have* to say that. It is a message dressed in the benefits of individual choice heralding the introduction of more and more areas of life where citizens have no choice but to make choices, as high-quality universal provision is brought to an end in sector after sector. Previously this took place under the guise of introducing private-sector 'efficiencies' and working practices, but since 2008 the rationality for such policies has largely migrated to 'austerity', the euphemism for embedding neoliberalism via the 'shock doctrine' of disaster capitalism (Klein, 2007).

The freedom of enforced choice is linked to responsibilities to be effective choosers within the market options on offer. However, even amongst those most able to resist the application of austerity, market mechanisms and consumer choice produce increasing anxiety as the degree of complexity involved in managing the everyday increases and the time available to manage it decreases. In their estimated two hours of 'free time' per day, the adults of the United Kingdom's middle-class, dual-income households must exercise informed choices about their finances, their children's education, their personal and professional development, their lifestyle health impacts etc. Whilst simultaneously being invited to participate in endless consultation exercises on how to implement new techniques and technologies, they had no part in originating.

Neoliberal ascendancy elevates discourses of the economic, the individual and free choice to the positions of renewed prominence in the context of a 'knowledge economy', where information and information workers are elevated to a position of prominence once enjoyed by the 'commanding heights' of the industrial economy – such as miners and car workers. Perfect competition within this model continues to be underpinned by belief in the possibility of perfect knowledge, a possibility increasingly promoted through the elision of knowledge and information. This naive doctrine dismissed all counter factual argument through the There Is No Alternative (TINA) principle, which in effect asserts the primacy of market rationality in all spheres of life. The relationships between knowledge, power and information thus assume positions of central analytical importance in terms of public trust in the institutions of 'representative democracy' that are increasingly subordinated to the vagaries of bond markets, credit rating agencies and unelected global decisional fora.

The intended and unintended collective consequences of global neoliberalism are most evident, however, to those individuals least able to insulate themselves and their dependents against the negative impacts of modernisation. Gradually the degrees of separation between those labouring in the 'developed' and 'developing' world are reduced, as the global flows of material and immaterial production go into reverse siphoning jobs to the 'developing' economies. Couple this with austerity measures, a reducing tax take from corporate entities utilising offshore tax havens and the declaration of profits in low-tax zones and the result is widespread social and economic dislocation. As in all phases of transition between modes of production associated with intense techno-scientific innovation, there is a rise in 'poor people's movements' (Fox-Piven, 1979), those marginal social actors who are increasingly dispossessed and disenfranchised. Amongst such groups, withdrawal represents a strategy of resistance. Thus, material acts of withdrawal such as withholding labour have extended to immaterial acts such as the withdrawal of trust. Of course, the pervasive withdrawal of trust was a major feature in the 'hollowing out' of Soviet 'communism' as active expressions of 'living in truth' developed amongst dissident networks.

Unlike previous instances, this 'exodus' exists in a network society (Castells, 1996, 2012) that significantly transforms the possible axes of solidarity, the density and dispersal of information, and the density and dispersal of individuals/actors in novel ways. The discrete, constituent nation states of international relations become inhabited by significant diaspora communities. These communities experience the acts of discrete states towards their homelands both as denizens of the perpetrator state(s) and via social media as 'distanciated' members of the target states through familial and friendship networks and social media, as well as more formal media channels.

The outsider/insider/other nexus central to the imagined community and identity of nationhood becomes attenuated and the task of constituting boundary conditions infinitely more complex. Put another way, difference becomes increasingly manifest and omnipresent at precisely the moment in which a return to the 'core values' of 'citizenship' is foregrounded as one potential response to increasing social tensions. Freedom of speech, association and assembly – corner stones of the enlightenment national bourgeois public sphere – and the right to civil disobedience (Habermas, 1985) become increasingly controlled by state authorities trying to address complex issues of inter-subjectivity, identity and political mobilisation.

CRISIS AS SHOCK AND OPPORTUNITY

This is the context in which a financial crisis, originally referred to as a 'credit crunch' in 2005–2006, led to the near collapse of the banking system because of the dramatic failure of the regulatory mechanisms for the banking sector and financial capital under the deregulation of neoliberal economic policy. Whilst giving evidence at the Congressional hearing in to the crisis, Alan Greenspan, the former Chairman of the US Federal Reserve, and arch exponent of neoliberal ideology, admitted he had 'made a mistake in presuming' that financial firms could regulate themselves. When asked by Henry Waxman, the committee Chairman, 'if you found that your view of the world, your ideology was not right, it was not working?' Greenspan replied, 'Absolutely, precisely… you know, that's precisely the reason I was shocked, because I have been going for 40 years or more with very considerable evidence that it was working exceptionally well.'

In due course, this crisis also overturned well-established neoliberal tropes, including the 'moral hazard' of state support, for failing enterprises and in turn precipitated one of the largest transfers of debt, from private-sector debt to sovereign debt, as state support was necessitated for banks that were too big to fail. According to the office of the Special

Inspector General for the Troubled Asset Relief Program (SIGTARP), the US government's total outgoings in bailouts was 3.3 trillion dollars, with 16.9 trillion of future protections guaranteed (http://www.usfederal-bailout.com/). This amounts to 113% of US GDP. In the United Kingdom, the government had to commit to the equivalent of 101% of GDP in terms of promised support for the banking sector. This transfer of debt from the private sector to the state hastened sovereign debt crises and led to the instigation of 'austerity' measures, which in the United Kingdom are presently transforming welfare provision and subjecting welfare claimants to ever more degrading and punitive forms of classification, whilst the pay and bonuses of those in the banking sector continue to rise.

This financial crisis was precipitated in part by the very process of economic globalisation neoliberals had advocated. At the beginning of the 2000s, international investors looking for a higher yield than was possible through relatively 'safe' investments such as US Treasury bonds prompted financial innovation on Wall Street. This 'huge pool' of global money led to investment banks designing mortgage-backed securities, thereby spreading systemic risk from the US housing market to the international financial system. In effect deregulation enabled banks to spread risk that they would previously have held on to – mortgage debt in this instance – through slicing and parcelling it and trading these 'asset-backed securities' on global financial markets. This circulated the risk, which was then further multiplied through specialist markets in insuring risk using financial instruments such as credit default swaps. There are a number of accessible and narrative accounts of this process and its outcomes (Lanchester, 2010; Tett, 2010), which are insightful, informative and illuminating, but at its heart there remains a simple dynamic – the requirement of capital to maximize value on investment. As the accumulation of value becomes ever more complex under the conditions of globalisation described above, the banking sector had in effect responded by falling back upon the direct extraction of profit from those who were most susceptible to the idea of the 'American dream' represented by home ownership and consumer lifestyles As David Graeber, a key activist and intellectual with Occupy Wall Street Movement, describes it:

> Wall Street's profits are no longer extracted from industry and commerce at all, but from speculation and 'financial services' which… turns out to be simply a shakedown operation: outright imperialism overseas, and colluding with the government at home to ensure that most Americans fall in to debt, and then extracting the money directly. (Khatib, Killjoy, & McGuire, 2012, pp. 428–429).

The social movement response to this realization crystallised in the call to 'Occupy Wall Street' on 17 September 2011, a call that was initially made by the Canadian magazine Adbusters.

OCCUPY THE CRISIS?

The Occupy movement's rapid growth and the particular dynamics of each localised instance of occupation have already been well-documented (Castells, 2012; Graeber, 2013; Khatib et al., 2012). The number of occupations in the United States is estimated to have been in the order of 600 (Castells, 2012, p. 163) and these included most of the major cities and many small towns and neighbourhoods. Occupy, of course, had a number of immediate precursors and many commentators link the Occupy movement to the movement of the *indignadas* or 15 May (15-M) movement in Spain that arose earlier in the year. This movement, in turn, inspired by events elsewhere in Tunisia and Egypt, mobilised in the midst of the EU crisis, as a response to crippling austerity measures which had led to approximately 50% of young people becoming unemployed. This movement used the occupation of public squares as a means to remain publicly and politically visible and after its first manifestation in large demonstrations in Madrid, Barcelona and Valencia spread to over 100 cities in Spain and then 800 worldwide (Castells, 2012, p. 113).

Whilst the global dynamics of occupation and revolt were undoubtedly significant, other commentators also point to the domestic political opportunity structure in the United States and the 'opening' afforded by the Wisconsin 'wave' of protests in early 2011 (Fithian, 2012, p. 381; Nichols, 2012). A huge mobilisation took place in Wisconsin between February and June involving protests of 100,000 people and the occupation of the State Capitol Building in Madison (http://www.defendwisconsin.org/). This was the result of the Republican Governor Scott Walker's plans to limit the collective bargaining rights of public sector workers and ultimately led him to face a recall vote, which was prompted by over nine hundred thousand signatories to the recall motion and was only the third time this had happened in US history. The mobilisation in Wisconsin was important in a number of ways; it demonstrated that the Republican right, backed by the Tea Party movement, would utilise the financial 'crisis' as a justification for further attacks on the public sector and its workers, and it also provided a very graphic illustration of the political possibility of occupying public buildings and public spaces. A repertoire of collective action, which, whilst not unprecedented in the United States, had not been a feature of contemporary politics and which was certainly an inspiration for some of the early occupiers (Nichols, 2012).

Whilst none of these precursors are explicitly anti-capitalist in their orientation, and these movements and their constituents, from the Wisconsin Wave to the Spanish indignadas, have myriad aims, desires and outcomes, my argument is that what unites them is a common rejection of neoliberalism as norm and as a consequence a questioning of the central precepts of contemporary capitalism. However, in order to make sense of the Occupy movement as anti-capitalist, it is essential to understand contemporary capitalism as far more than an economic system. It must be understood as a socio-cultural, political and ideological entity that is inextricably linked to the core institutions of Western modernity as well as to a universalising global spatiality, one which Occupy explicitly and materially contests. This in turn also requires recognising that past anti-capitalist approaches were premised on certain theoretical approaches and assumptions – most prominently Marxist-Leninism – that shared a great deal with the dominant political model of liberal modernity. Contemporary anti-capitalist movements are instead notable for rejecting centralised forms of power, universalising or homogenising visions of change, as well as theoretical approaches that are formulaic or dogmatic (Chesters & Welsh, 2006; Notes from Nowhere, 2003). Moreover, increasing awareness of the complicity of leftist approaches in ecological and cultural exploitation has inspired more ecologically oriented and culturally pluralist approaches to emerge.

In this context, the critique of neoliberal capitalism mounted by Occupy and its insistence on making visible the stakes of what would otherwise occur behind closed doors shares much with the AGM. This movement came into worldwide visibility with the anti-WTO protests in Seattle in November 1999 and is best known for its opposition to corporate-driven neoliberal globalisation and the multilateral institutions that enforce its policies – the G8, IMF, WTO and World Bank. Moreover, I suggest that beyond its critique and opposition to neoliberalism, the most significant and effective parts of the alter-globalisation movement are best understood to be anti-capitalist. This is, of course, contentious because many actors who identified with or participated in this movement do not necessarily define their practice or political ideology as anti-capitalist per se.

In fact, one of the notable things about the AGM is precisely its internal heterogeneity, including the diversity of political positions. However, even though there are many elements of the movement that are not consciously anti-capitalist, taken together the most important and significant aspects of the AGM are anti-systemic, and anti-capitalist, if not in their intent, then at least in their effects.

What ties this movement to more recent manifestations such as Occupy, in addition to their common histories and similar constituent organisations and actors, is a common political imaginary, one that can be referred to as anti- or post-capitalist. The three core elements of this imaginary are (a) a rejection of the notion of state power or party politics; (b) the foundational importance of difference and multiplicity and (c) critique, reflexivity and enquiry, rather than linear or formulaic dogmatisms. While comprehensible in and of themselves, these elements can be understood in large part as a contrast to, or a direct response to, politics past, even Marxist and leftist politics, which are equally inflected by the culture and values of Western modernity.

The praxis of Occupy reaffirms that 'space', its liberation, enclosure and use is a crucial subject and debate amongst movement actors. Rather than analyse movements through the crucial categories of identity and ideology or measure their success according to specific objectives – some have posited an understanding of movements as creating 'spaces of politicization' (Mezzadra, 2003). The centrality of space also relates to the possibilities for encounters across difference, the clash or convergence of the unexpected, and is radically distinct from the dominant view of the aim and goals of political movements. The fact that capitalism was enabled through the enclosures of the commons makes it quite apt that the liberation and occupation of space for alternative, anti-capitalist futures should be a prominent strategy. However, the use and enclosure of space by capitalism also continues. For example, the concept of enclosure, whilst echoing traditional protest themes, can be extended to include the increased penetration and control of social spaces by capitalist interests. As well as the extension of disciplinary and surveillance apparatus into all spheres of life, from the flow of information and commonly produced creative goods to the commodification of the very materiality of existence through bio and nano-technologies. Similarly, as Native Americans have pointed out to the Occupy Wall Street Movement, all of these occupations are themselves on land that was itself occupied.

Debates around the political efficaciousness of taking, occupying or simply inhabiting space point to some of the more subtle, yet key, differences amongst various anti-capitalist positions. In particular, between those who see the symbolic use of space as part and parcel of the political aim and those who see the symbolic use of space as space-holder until real political power and impact are attained. Particular attention is paid, by those within the Occupy movement to the role of the state in this 'dialogue' between capital and civil society and its increasing tendency to act as the enforcer for capitalist interests.

CONCLUSION: FROM OCCUPY THE CITY TO RECONSTRUCTING THE COMMONS

In addition to the articulation and capture of spaces for resistance to neoliberalism, some amongst the Occupy movement now see their actions as asserting the primacy of the 'commons' and 'commoning' (Dyer-Witheford, 2009; Patel, 2009) against the corporate enclosure of social life and the increasingly fragile existence of 'public spaces' that are in practice spaces opened and closed by the state (Res-publica). This was particularly evident in the way in which many of the occupations were ended, with local government and police forces often relying upon the use of comparatively minor local ordinances to restrict public access to otherwise 'public' spaces. This manipulation of public access through the enforcement of minor regulations has led some to suggest that the 'biopolitical' control of the contemporary urban environment has also been revealed by the occupiers (Caffentzis, 2012), revealing how the concept of the commons, which many presumed underpinned their use of these public spaces, is actually a subversive desire in the neoliberal city. It is of little surprise then that since the end of the camps, many of those who were involved have turned their attention to forms of 'commoning' that evoke different uses of urban space, organising to resist evictions, organise debt strikes, re-wild urban spaces, or to participate in guerrilla gardening and form intentional communities of 'commoners'.

These concerns are indicative of the alternative political imaginaries that have emerged over the last 2–3 decades of anti-capitalist mobilisation. They reflect the interesting fusion of anarchist, autonomist and ecological insights that have been posited as a response to the systemic crises of the environment, democracy and the economy that underlie most social and political anxieties. The question of whether the concept and practice of 'the commons' can really redress the paucity of political alternatives under the politics as usual of liberal democratic states is a challenging one. However, the mass experiments in agency, deliberation, participation and social relations that have constituted contemporary anti-capitalism, from social forums to the convergence spaces of Occupy, the utopian engagement with alternative land use and the creative resistance of hacker collectives and data dumpers suggests at the very least there are some causes for optimism.

The focus for many activists who have been at the heart of Occupy is now on the challenges of building alternative commons and communities among diverse networks comprised of divergent cultural orientations and worldviews. Of course, the challenge of the collective and communal are well known to social theorists, anthropologists, historians of socialist and post-socialist societies, as well as experienced activists. The question then becomes what new tools, ideas and strategies are being proposed and debated to re-imagine and recreate 'commoning' as a more viable and durable practice? Moreover, how do practices of 'commoning' interact with mainstream or non-mobilised parts of societies? How does a politics of commoning deal with elections, the state and society at large?

These are questions around which there is already a significant debate and many proposals, including calls to 'Occupy money' (Kennedy, 2012), or indeed democracy, through systems of participatory engagement based upon movement learning derived from the assemblies, forums, and spokes councils of Occupy and beyond (Graeber, 2013; Sitrin & Azellini, 2013). What many have noted is that whilst the media attention might have waned with the eviction of the camps and the squares, and the institutional narrative might be one of failure, this movement has moved in to a different phase, one sometimes described in the literature as a 'latency phase'. The social movement theorist Alberto Melucci differentiated between the political significance of social movements that tends to be assessed through the study of visible interventions and the social and cultural significance of movements that are latent activities. This latent portion of movement activity takes place at the 'molecular' level of day-to-day social relations and is central in constituting collective identities capable of resistance and conflict. For Melucci 'the latency of a movement is its effective strength' (1989, p. 71). Whilst Occupy is entering a latency *phase*, it is also an outcome of a latency *period* that culminated in the emergence of the alter-globalisation movement in the early 1990s as movements of the North and South began to explicitly express their opposition to neoliberal capitalism.

In countries with established welfare states associated with commitments to full employment and collective provision to meet social needs through state-run agencies, neoliberalism represented a particularly acute and systemic challenge to all forms of social movement 'old' and 'new'. The common challenge of neoliberalism was experienced by movements in both the

Northern and Southern hemispheres heralding the start of a latency period lasting several years. In this latency period the work of (re)defining the collective stakes for societies reshaped by the neoliberal project occurred within movement milieu. As Melucci argues, these latency periods are part of the process through which movements 'join past and future' by reconfiguring the demands and concerns of past movements and situating them in the present. This is a process of negotiation and conflict through which individuals and groups construct, adjust and express the multiple forces that might constitute a contemporary field of collective action through reflection upon and engagement with the past (Melucci, 1996, pp. 351–355). Advances in computer-mediated communications increased the connectivity between a diverse range of movement actors that identified neoliberalism as a 'common enemy' (Castells, 1997) and consolidated into the alternative globalisation movement during this period (Chesters & Welsh, 2006).

The crisis of accumulation arising from neoliberal deregulation and profit maximisation in 2007–2008 is likely to mark the onset of another latency period as past and future are renegotiated in the context of the shock doctrine of unpayable debt. As Occupy disperses from the physical spaces of the City, we are challenged by its declaration of the stakes involved in this new moment and its call to engage with the distinctive features of the political imaginary it manifested. To create a distinct culture of politics that re-envisions forms of power, sees difference as central and valuable and inheres a commitment to creative, reflexive and on-going critique. An imaginary contrasted with the formulaic dogmatisms of classical anti-capitalist thought and the institutional limitations of representative democracy.

NOTE

1. It was resistance to the plan to build a shopping mall on Taksm Gezi Park that sparked a more general uprising against the Erdogan government in Turkey in May 2013.

REFERENCES

Caffentzis, G. (2012). In Desert Cities. In K. Khatib, M. Killjoy & M. McGuire (Eds.), *We are many: Reflections on movement strategy from occupation to liberation.* Edinburgh: AK Press.

Castells, M. (1996). *The Rise of the network society, Vol. 1, The information age: Economy, society and culture*. Oxford: Blackwell.
Castells, M. (1997). *The power of identity: The information age: Economy, society, and culture* (Vol. 2). Oxford: Blackwell.
Castells, M. (2012). *Networks of outrage and hope: Social movements in the internet age*. Cambridge: Polity.
Chesters, G., & Welsh, I. (2006). *Complexity and social movements: Multitudes at the edge of chaos*. London: Routledge.
Crouch, C. (2013). *The Strange non-death of neoliberalism*. Cambridge: Polity.
Davis, M., & Monk, D. (2009). *Evil paradises: Dreamworlds of neoliberalism*. New York, NY: The New Press.
Dyer-Witheford, N. (2009). 'Commonism', *Turbulence*, 1. Retrieved from: http://turbulence.org.uk/turbulence-1/commonism/
Escobar, A. (2008). *Territories of difference: Place, movements, life, redes*. Durham, NC: Duke University Press.
Fithian, L. (2012). Strategic directions for the occupy movement. In K. Khatib, M. Killjoy & M. McGuire (Eds.), *We are many: Reflections on movement strategy from occupation to liberation*. Edinburgh: AK Press.
Fox-Piven, F. (1979). *Poor peoples' movements: Why they succeed, how they fail*. New York, NY: Random House.
Graeber, D. (2013). *The Democracy project: A history, a crisis, a movement*. London: Penguin.
Habermas, J. (1985). Civil disobedience: The Litmus test for the democratic constitutional state. *Berkeley Journal of Sociology*, *30*, 95–116.
Hardt, M., & Negri, A. (2000). *Empire*. Cambridge, MA: Harvard University Press.
Harvey, D. (2007). *A Brief history of neoliberalism*. Oxford: Oxford University Press.
Hattenstone, S. (2011). Mark Kennedy: Confessions of an Undercover Cop. *The Guardian*, 26 March. Retrieved from http://www.guardian.co.uk/environment/2011/mar/26/mark-kennedy-undercover-cop-environmental-activist
Hutton, W. (2002). *The world we're In*. London: Little Brown.
Kennedy, M. (2012). *Occupy money: Creating an economy where everybody wins*. London: New Society Publishers.
Khatib, K., Killjoy, M, & McGuire, M. (eds.). (2012). *We are many: Reflections on movement strategy from occupation to liberation*. Edinburgh: AK Press.
Klein, N. (2007). *The shock doctrine: The Rise of disaster capitalism*. New York, NY: Metropolitan Books.
Lanchester, J. (2010). *Whoops!: Why everyone owes everyone and no one can pay*. London: Penguin Books.
Larsson, B., Letell, M., & Thorn, H. (2012). *Transformations of the swedish welfare state: From social engineering to Governance?* London: Palgrave.
McCormack. (1991). The Price of influence: The Political economy of Japanese leisure. *New Left Review*, *188*, 121–134.
Melucci, A. (1989). *Nomads of the present*. London: Radius Hutchinson.
Melucci, A. (1996). *Challenging codes: Collective action in the information age*. Cambridge: Cambridge University Press.
Mezzadra, S. (2003). Luoghi Comuni: il movimento globale come spazio de politicizazione. *Derive Approdi*, *24*, 2–6.

Nichols, J. (2012). *Uprising: How wisconsin renewed the politics of protest, from madison to wall street*. New York, NY: Perseus.

Notes from Nowhere. (Eds.). (2003). *We are everywhere: The irresistible rise of global anticapitalism*. London: Verso.

Patel, R. (2009). *The Value of nothing: How to reshape market society and redefine democracy*. London: Picador.

Rodrik, D. (2011). *The Globalization paradox: Why global markets, states and democracy can't coexist*. Oxford: Oxford University Press.

Sitrin, M. & Azellini, D. (2013) *Occupying language: The secret rendezvous with history and the present*. New York, NY: Zucotti Park Press.

Stedman-Jones, D. (2012). *Masters of the universe: Hayek, friedman, and the birth of neoliberal politics*. Princeton, NJ: Princeton University Press.

Stiglitz, J. (2007). *Making globalisation work*. New York, NY: W. W. Norton & Company.

Tett, G. (2010). *Fool's Gold: How unrestrained greed corrupted a dream, shattered global markets and unleashed a catastrophe*. London: Abacus.

Welsh, I. (2000). *Mobilising modernity: The Nuclear moment*. London: Routledge.

CIVIL SOCIETY, THE LEFT AND COMMUNITY ORGANISING: TOWARDS A PROGRESSIVE POLITICS

Paul Bunyan

ABSTRACT

Purpose – *This chapter reviews critically the policy developments in the United Kingdom since 2010 with the adoption by the coalition of 'community organising' as both a concept and practice.*

Design – *The chapter is an extensive literature review informed by critical thinking and reflection.*

Findings – *The chapter argues that the model adopted in the United Kingdom is unlikely to address the power imbalances between civil society organisations and the state and that there needs to be a more critical and reflective assessment of the potential of civil society agencies to influence public policy in a progressive way.*

Implications/originality: – *The chapter is intentionally speculative.*

Keywords: Alinsky; civil society; community organising; London citizens

Looking for Consensus?: Civil Society, Social Movements and Crises for Public Management
Critical Perspectives on International Public Sector Management, Volume 2, 123–138

ISSN: 2045-7944/doi:10.1108/S2045-7944(2013)0000002009

INTRODUCTION

The banking collapse and global financial crisis of recent years raises important questions about human agency and the extent to which people in their localities and institutions can in any way challenge or resist such structural forces. Despite the scale and impact of the crisis, the state–market nexus, which from the 1970s onwards advanced neo-liberal forms of capitalism throughout much of the world, has remained intact. In the face of what would appear to be overbearing economic and political forces, attention has turned towards civil society both in terms of its potential to ameliorate the effects of the crisis and in more radical terms challenge neo-liberal hegemony.

This chapter considers this turn towards civil society and the possibilities for a progressive politics bringing together interests from the Left and civil society to challenge neo-liberal hegemony. Adherents of the Left and civil society are of course not mutually exclusive – many within civil society, whether overtly political or not, would subscribe to a politics more left than right, more socialist than individualist, more state- than market-oriented. However, in terms of people's institutional loyalties, their associational activities and how they expend their energies and resources, a distinction can be drawn between those who are more civil society-oriented than state-oriented and vice versa. The first part of the chapter examines the nature of the relationship between the Left and civil society. Historically, it has been the state which has been the almost exclusive focus and concern of the Left in considering social and political change. Drawing upon recent analysis by Richard Sennett, the ambivalence that has often marked the left's stance towards civil society as a credible locus of social and political change is examined. The second part of the chapter focuses on community organising as an approach to developing agency and building power within civil society. In the United Kingdom, community organising has divided opinion amongst activists on the left, many of whom see it as a form of communitarianism and a distraction to the fundamental task of securing state-led solutions to issues of social justice. Its association in recent years with the 'Big Society', the flagship policy idea of the Conservative Party's 2010 general election manifesto, has served to confirm suspicion that the focus upon civil society and community organising represents nothing more than a mask for the public cuts implemented by the coalition government. The argument set forth in this chapter is that a new progressive politics is required which both recognises the role of the state in creating the social, economic and political conditions for a fair and just society but also the critical role of civil society in contesting state and market power and pushing the boundaries of civility and social justice. Despite its limitations, it is argued that community organising provides an important vehicle for developing a progressive politics capable of aligning interests from the Left and civil society to contest the public sphere and to challenge neo-liberal hegemony.

Neo-Liberal Co-Option of 'Civil Society'

It is important to start with an analysis of the ways in which, what Harvey (2005) has termed 'the neo-liberal state', promoted both by New Labour and the current Conservative-led coalition, commandeered terms such as 'civil society', 'community' and 'partnership' to political narratives which consolidated neo-liberal hegemony and promoted a consensus-based understanding of social and political change. For New Labour in 1997 the narrative was about a 'Third Way', charting a course between the state and market, and linked to this the notion of 'partnership' between the state, market and civil society. The market, under Thatcherism, had brought increased prosperity for many but at the expense of increasing inequality throughout society at large. Distancing itself from the past and the party's perceived enmity towards the market, part of what the 'new' in New Labour was designed to project, was a political project that countenanced – some might say embraced – the market, albeit within a regulatory framework which was meant to curb the market's natural propensity towards excess (history has not been kind in this regard and Gordon Brown on his defeat as New Labour leader in the 2010 general election, perhaps not surprisingly, remarked that his greatest regret was not regulating the market more). Partnership was the hallmark of the Third Way. On assuming power, New Labour very quickly courted the so-called 'Third Sector' or civil society, proclaiming partnership between the state, market and civil society as the way forward in promoting effective social, economic and political change

For the Conservatives in the run up to the 2010 election, the narrative or 'big idea' was the 'Big Society'. The market had clearly failed, plunging the country into economic, political and social crisis. However, as the party most closely associated with the market, the Conservatives developed what turned out to be an effective political narrative which sought to deflect attention away from market failure, blaming New Labour's profligacy in managing the economy and creating a bloated state, as the primary reason for the crisis. In terms of the 'solution' (or at least an important part of the solution), the Conservatives, like New Labour over a decade before, turned to civil society. According to Cameron New Labour's focus upon the state had disenfranchised local communities – the Big Society would shift power away from the state towards civil society, empowering people to take more responsibility for their communities, including the provision of public services previously delivered by the state.

A parallel can be drawn here between New Labour's focus upon 'partnership' and the Conservatives take on the 'Big Society' (Bunyan, 2013). Underpinning the rhetoric of both 'partnership' and the 'Big Society' is the assumption of a shift in power away from the state and market towards civil society. In fact the opposite has largely been the case. Under neo-liberalism the state–market nexus retained control putting in place 'managerial technologies' and governance arrangements which significantly constrained the practices of civil society or third sector organisations. For example, under New Labour and 'partnership' the Third Sector was radically reshaped and restructured:

> Large voluntary organizations became quasi-governmental in nature, taking on large-scale services previously undertaken by the state, while smaller voluntary organizations, through commissioning processes, were brought much more under the controlling auspices of the state. This effectively led to a 'hollowing out' and depoliticization of much of the third sector. (Bunyan, 2013, p. 123)

Glasman, in his analysis of the impact of the state–market nexus upon civil society, sees it as being fundamentally detrimental. He says:

> If the state becomes the ultimate source of collective power and the market that of money, then it is not surprising that society – the third sphere, and source of reciprocity and association – finds itself impoverished and powerless. As self-funded dues-paying associations become weaker, the institutions of society become increasingly dependent on the state and the market, and so are less capable of pursuing their own interests and values. (Glasman, 2010, p. 59)

Language has played a fundamental role in the entrenchment of neo-liberalism. Garrett (2009), in his analysis of the 'transformation' of children's services, draws attention to how power relations operate through language and how keywords often imperceptibly contribute to the solidifying of neoliberal hegemony. Examples of such keywords and terms include 'flexibility', 'empowerment', 'partnership', 'Big Society', 'social entrepreneur' etc. Quoting Harvey, such language, according to Garrett, shapes the way we see the world and accept change, becoming 'so embedded in common sense as to be taken for granted and not open to question' (Harvey, 2005, p. 5).

The Left and Civil Society

In an article entitled 'A Creditable Left' published in *The Nation* in August 2011, sociologist, philosopher and self-confessed 'Lefty' Richard Sennett reflects upon the collapse of the financial system in 2008 as well as his hopes that it might have heralded a rising up against the 'Capitalist Beast', as governments and voters moved to the left in response. That this didn't materialise causes Sennett to ponder on the predicament faced by activists on the left today. He says,

> The unpalatable fact is that we, the ardent Left, count for less and less in the public's thinking about how to live together. And if that has long been true in the United States, where the Left has occupied only a small corner of public discourse, the decay of the left now marks the old Western European homelands, as in Sweden or Britain. The word 'progressive' seems no more arousing than 'social democracy'. Though progressive think tanks abound in America and Europe, and churn out worthy proposals for social justice, policy-wonkery seems to induce an eyes-glazed-over indifference among the larger public. (2011, p. 24)

In thinking about how the Left can become more creditable in people's eyes, Sennett sees the problem as being more social than ideological. 'Creditability', he comments, 'lies more in the realm of receptiveness than assertiveness' (p. 24). By this, Sennett infers that those on the left have to be less concerned with winning an argument and more concerned with getting alongside people – understanding the importance of 'presence' in politics – to discuss on equal terms issues that matter and how best to live. Sennett believes a certain kind of politics follows – 'It should concentrate more on civil society than electoral politics – particularly electoral politics at the national level' (p. 24).

Historically, tensions have long existed on the left about the value of civil society in thinking about social and political change. Marx was dismissive of civil society seeing it as a camouflage for the domination of the capitalist class (Alexander, 2006). It was Gramsci, a later disciple of Marx, who recognised, in his concept of hegemony, the contingent nature of social and political change and the potential of civil society to impact the existing relations of power. According to Powell, Gramsci recognised that social change had to be negotiated democratically – it could not come about solely by the capture or imposition of the state. As Powell (2007, p. 81) says, 'The

Jacobin–Bolshevik belief that revolution could be secured by storming the citadel of power was redundant.'

Sennett, in the aforementioned article draws attention to divisions between adherents of the Left going back over a century. He says,

> There's nothing new about arguing that we should pay more attention to a socially oriented, community building politics in civil society. By the dawn of the twentieth century, the left had divided in two: a political left that focused on elections and dealings with government, and a social left involved with mutual support in settlement houses, cooperative banks and other voluntary associations. The two sides confronted each other in 1900 at the Paris Universal Exposition, in a set of rooms devoted to 'The Social Question'; here, the political left displayed various manifestoes for government reform and the organization of unions, while the social left showed photographs of the streets and buildings where community organizers worked. Despite both sides' agreement on the evils of capitalism, they talked past each other on how to respond: the political left, represented by German trade unions, accused its opponents of lacking the discipline and strength that should adhere in mass movements; the social left, spoken for by American settlement-house workers, argued that only face-to-face co-operation, no matter how informal or messy, could rescue immigrants and other people from isolation in cities. One side sought adherence to policy; the other saw politics as beginning with engagement, empathy and trust-building. (Sennett, 2011, p. 25)

The divisions highlighted by Sennett have continued to the present day as the power of both the political left and social left has been steadily eroded. The political left – the unions and the modern Labour party – has failed to maintain and develop links to poor and working-class localities and communities that once existed. The agenda of the social left, or what might be referred to today as civil society or the Third Sector, has in recent decades increasingly been directed by the state and the shift towards state-funded service delivery. In the process, the social left has lost much of its independence and political efficacy. The current plight of both the political left and social left – the former increasingly remote and 'hollowed out', the latter increasingly neutralised – is a lethal cocktail for poor and working-class communities who have traditionally looked to the Left to protect them from the excesses of the market and to advance their interests politically.

In thinking about the current plight of the Left and of the possibilities of a new and progressive form of politics, an important point can be extrapolated from the preceding analysis which relates to the issue of structure and agency. It is that whilst an understanding of the structural forces which blight the lives of individuals and communities is an important prerequisite to thinking about human agency, the development of an effective strategy to build such agency and contest such forces, particularly with poor and working-class people, is a much more difficult and complex task particularly within the hostile context of neo-liberal hegemony. Put another way, whilst the Left has often been strong on structure – for example, a Marxist interpretation of the current economic crisis by an author such as David Harvey remains the most compelling and incisive of analyses – it has been less surefooted, increasingly so in recent times, on the issue of human agency and developing effective strategies at a grass-roots level to contest social and political change. Admittedly, there are no ready or easy 'solutions' to the question of human agency. In modern-day politics, in which the media plays an increasingly important role and the focus is primarily on what happens at Westminster, the question of whether much attention, time and resources should be devoted by political parties to the local and to developing the 'presence' referred to by Sennett is a legitimate one. The answer, of course, is that it matters a great deal – declining democratic participation and the hollowing out of the body politic is more serious for the Left than the Right. Capitalist consumerism and the increasing individualisation and atomisation of society impacts the rich less, who can ride out economic crises and use their resources and contacts to secure and retain power, than the poor, who suffer disproportionately, particularly in times of austerity, and who can only build power through collective action. If the Left is going to be seen as creditable in the eyes of poor people then the attention and focus, as Sennett suggests, will need to shift from power conceived top-down and almost exclusively in electoral terms, to the complex and challenging task of building power from the bottom-up in localities and communities.

Community Organising and Power

Community organising originated in the United States and derives from the work of Saul Alinsky, who from the 1940s till his death in 1972 built a reputation as one of America's most controversial and radical organizers, credited with changing urban politics and influencing future leaders including President Barack Obama and Hillary Clinton. In the 1940s, Alinsky established the Industrial Areas Foundation (IAF) to promote community organising across the United States – the IAF remains today at the forefront of community organising working in more than 60 cities across the United States with affiliates in Australia, Canada, Germany and the United Kingdom. In 1989, the Citizen Organising Foundation, now Citizens UK, was formed to develop community organising in the United

Kingdom. Close links were established with the IAF, whose experienced organisers helped to train the first small group of community organisers in the early 1990s. It is beyond the scope of this chapter to chart the development of community organising in the United Kingdom since the early 1990s – for a critical perspective of the challenges and issues involved in establishing community organising within a UK context and of the philosophy and principles underpinning an Alinskyan approach see the article 'Broad-based organising in the UK: Reasserting the centrality of political activity in community development' (Bunyan, 2010). Suffice to say that after a difficult initial period in the 1990s when community organising struggled to become established, from 2000 onwards it firmly took root and grew in profile, most notably through the work of London Citizens, the main affiliate of the national body Citizens UK. The profile was raised further in 2010 when David Cameron announced during the General Election campaign that upon election community organising would form part of the strategy to help build the so-called Big Society.

The association of community organising with the Big Society, as highlighted in the introduction, led many on the left to dismiss the approach and the shift in focus towards civil society as little more than a mask for public sector cuts. In an article published in 2010 entitled 'Society not State: The Challenge of the Big Society,' Maurice Glasman, an advocate of community organising and the architect of ideas associated with what has been termed 'Blue Labour' (reported in 2009 by Guardian journalist Allegra Stratton as 'a new politics of reciprocity, mutuality and solidarity'), appealed to proponents of the left to not too readily dismiss the idea of the Big Society. He says,

> It is important that the Big Society is not dismissed as trivial. It addresses important issues relating to the redistribution of power and democracy – a necessary part of a renewed progressive politics – and provides a basis for public sector reform that is linked to greater employee ownership and a diversity of provision. It is consciously political, in that it seeks to provoke a reactive statism among its progressive opponents, thus stifling their capacity to address the weaknesses of New Labour in office and renew the public policy on the left. (Glasman, 2010, p. 62)

The problem with Cameron's interpretation of the Big Society, as Glasman went on to say in the article, is that for all the rhetoric directed against the state very little is said about the market. No acknowledgement is given to the tensions between a commitment to the political economy of neo-liberalism which encourages mobility, flexibility and competitiveness and the sense of place and stable association necessary for people to build an active community life based upon values of mutuality and solidarity. In his challenge to the Left Glasman concludes:

> The significance of Big Society lies in the possibilities it opens up for progressives to develop an agenda that combines democratic renewal, market and state accountability and a politics of citizenship that the previous government did not seize in office. In order to do this, progressives need to reconceptualise their approach to diversity, devolution and democracy, and reclaim progressive traditions of mutuality and cooperation. It will not be possible to take on market power without the interests of an active organised society. (Glasman, 2010, p. 62)

This last point about the need for an active, organised society to take on market power is central to the development of a progressive politics. Community organising, I maintain, provides a coherent philosophy and approach for people in their localities and communities to begin to build a platform to contest existing configurations of power. But in order for this to happen, a clear distinction needs to be made between an authentic community-organising approach, recognizable in concrete terms by its impact on existing relations of power at a local and broader institutional level, and other community-based approaches which do not deliver in the same terms. A radical and authentic community organising approach, I have argued:

- recognizes power as the central organising issue;
- understands that social change and social justice are as much about struggle, tension and conflict as they are about consensus and co-operation; and
- incorporates a strategy that, while based in the local, aims to transcend it and engage people collectively at a broader institutional level (Bunyan, 2013, p. 130).

Currently, four distinct community organising initiatives can be identified in the United Kingdom:

1. Citizens UK, the longest running and largest network in terms of profile, member organisations, track record and campaigns.
2. The government sponsored community organising programme, run by the organisation Locality and aimed at training up to five thousand community organisers over the course of the current parliament.
3. Movement for Change, founded by David Milliband in the aftermath of the 2010 General Election, designed to revitalise the Labour party at a local level by focusing upon community-based politics. The website describes Movement for Change as 'the home of community organising in the Labour movement' and interestingly both London Citizens and

the Industrial Areas Foundation were instrumental in providing the initial training for the team of community organisers spearheading the initiative within the party. For an excellent account of the politics surrounding the development of 'Movement for Change', the ideas associated with what has been termed 'Blue Labour' and the influence of Citizens UK in helping to develop community organising within the Labour party, see journalist Rowenna Davis's book *Tangled up in Blue: Blue Labour and the Struggle for Labour's Soul*, published in 2011.

4. Powered by People UK, supported by Church Action on Poverty and currently involving initiatives, relatively small in scale at this point, in Manchester, Teesside, North Wales and Birmingham.

It is too early to tell how many of the initiatives which come under the banner of 'community organising' will measure up against the criteria identified above and develop sufficient power to play a significant role in the public and political life of localities, cities and regions of the United Kingdom. At this stage only Citizens UK, in particular its main affiliate London Citizens, could lay claim to such an influence. As such it is worth looking briefly at some of the key features of London Citizens, now the largest broad-based community organisation in the United Kingdom, and the way in which the organisation has managed to build power and become a significant player in the politics and public life of the Capital. Three areas, in particular, deserve attention – first, the institutional basis of the organisation; second, the nature of the organisation's campaigns and third, the role of the community organiser.

First, and most importantly, in terms of its agency and power, is London Citizen's institutional-based membership which now numbers almost 200 member organisations across London. This includes faith institutions, universities, colleges, schools, trade unions and community groups. The structure of London Citizens, member organisations, organised in four chapters, covering North, South, West and East London, allows for different levels of democratic participation and engagement by members at a local, borough and citywide level. Saul Alinsky, the founder of community organising, referred to earlier, understood that whilst on the surface the problems associated with poor communities were often presented in terms of needs, the underlying causes and how they were to be addressed was fundamentally to do with power. Alinsky's great insight was that in poor communities, institutions such as faith groups, unions and other community-based organisations, represented what Alex de Tocqueville, once referred to as 'little platoons', associations that could be brought together and harnessed to build a more powerful broad-based institution. According to Alinsky, in 'Reveille for Radicals', first published in 1946:

> The purpose of the organization should be interpreted as proposing to deal with those major issues which no one single agency is – or can be – big or strong enough to cope with. Then each agency will continue to carry out its own program, but all are being banded together to achieve sufficient strength to cope with issues that are so vast and deep that no one or two community agencies would ever consider tackling them. (Alinsky, 1989, p. 87)

Second, in terms of building the power and profile of London Citizens has been the organisation's ability to move between small-scale localised campaigns – for example, negotiating a road sign from the council or a 'green man' for a dangerous crossing – to broader strategic campaigns at a citywide level – for example the Living Wage which has grown to become a successful national campaign. It was the Living Wage campaign, initiated in 2001 by The East London Communities Organisation (TELCO), the first chapter and forerunner of London Citizens, which most significantly raised the profile of community organising, bringing into membership, local union branches and building alliances with some of the major national unions, most notably Unite. At times this was not without its tensions – at first there was resistance from many in the unions who saw the campaign instigated by an organisation, whose membership was predominantly faith-based, as an unwelcome intrusion on to territory that was theirs. By the same token, seeking an alliance with unions, the epitomy of the Left, inviting the possibility of a shift in the culture of the organisation, was for some within membership of TELCO at the time, a potential risk and represented in many ways an act of faith, both literally and metaphorically. In terms of the argument presented in this chapter and the need for a new and progressive politics the Living Wage campaign represents an important example of the way in which new alliances can be built, in this case between faith, labour and community, to work for social and political change.

Finally, the role of community organisers has been essential in building and sustaining London Citizens over a period of almost two decades. The primary role of the professional community organiser is to build what Alinsky termed 'native leadership'. Describing the role and mindset of the organiser Miller (2010) says:

> Professional organizers focus on building community and power. Issues are simply tools for the building process. What is won is no doubt important. But the organizer's questions, and increasingly the questions of a growing core of committed leaders, have to do with changing the relations of power: How did our leaders grow in self-confidence? What did they learn? Which new people assumed leadership responsibilities? Are

> they going to continue in these roles? Who are new recruits or potential recruits? What relationships were developed or deepened in our constituency? How was our reputation enhanced? What new allies were made? Have we gained respect from power structure figures who will now negotiate with us differently? Are new fundraising possibilities available? How about media?

Neil Jameson, the executive director of London Citizens, has been this country's leading proponent and most effective community organiser. Jameson first arrived in East London in 1995 to start building TELCO. Building and sustaining an organisation the size to which London Citizens has now grown represents one of the the most ambitious and successful experiments in democracy that the United Kingdom has seen over the past two decades. This is down largely to Jameson and the team of organisers, now numbering over twenty that have taken the lead in building the organisation over that period.

Community organising and the approach adopted by London Citizens and its national body, Citizens UK, are best understood essentially as an urban strategy. Density of local institutions, diversity of communities, development of a multi-issue agenda and, importantly, access to independent sources of money, most notably from charitable Trusts and Foundations (many of which are based in major cities and are oriented in their work towards disadvantaged areas), are the conditions in which such organisations are most likely to take root and prosper. The main challenge for Citizens UK over the next decade is to replicate the success of the work in London in other cities and areas across the United Kingdom. Currently, there are organisations in Birmingham, Nottingham and Milton Keynes and a sponsoring committee, which represents the initial stage of building an organisation tasked with raising the funds to employ a community organizer, have also been established in Glasgow and Cardiff.

Towards a Progressive Politics

In their analysis of socialist strategy and call for a new form of radical and plural democratic politics, Laclau and Mouffe point to the contingent nature of what they term 'the social', that is, society, and the possibilities for a new hegemonic strategy of the Left. They say,

> It is not in the abandonment of the democratic terrain but, on the contrary, in the extension of the field of democratic struggles to the whole of civil society and the state that the possibility resides for a hegemonic strategy of the Left. It is nevertheless important to understand the radical extent of the changes which are necessary in the political

> imaginary of the Left, if it wishes to succeed in founding a political practice fully located in the field of the democratic revolution and conscious of the depth and variety of the hegemonic articulations which the present conjuncture requires. (2001, p. 176)

The authors highlight a number of obstacles which in their view seriously limits the Left's capacity for action and political analysis. First, statism –'the idea that the expansion of the role of the state is the panacea for all problems' (p. 177); second, classism – 'the idea that the working class represents the privileged agent in which the fundamental impulse of social change resides' (p. 177); thirdly, revolution, understood in the Jacobin mould, that is, the idea that power could be seized in a decisive moment or event 'from which society could be "rationally" reorganised' (p. 177). In questioning these tenets of leftist thinking, Laclau and Mouffe's central argument is that social change and radical democracy needs to be conceived in terms of a plurality of struggles: 'The multiplication of political spaces and the preventing of power in one point are then preconditions of every truly democratic transformation of society' (p. 178).

In advocating a move away from essentialist thinking which conceives of social change in a particular way, that is, in terms of state, class and revolution, Laclau and Mouffe challenge the Left to think in more expansive terms about how to combat what they term the 'anti-democratic offensive' embodied in recent times by neo-liberal hegemony. To this end, they contend, it is both the state and civil society which should be conceived as the terrain upon which human agency and the multiplication of political spaces and democratic struggles are to be developed.

A fundamental question which follows from Laclau and Mouffe's analysis concerns the extent to which people who are different and belong to different types of organisations and institutions can find common ground to act in concert and develop power. Sennett's analysis about the current plight of the Left in the article published in *The Nation* in 2011 was followed by a book in 2012 entitled *Together: The Rituals, Pleasures and Politics of Co-operation,* in which he examines the nature of and potential for co-operation between people who differ. Part of the conundrum for Sennett is how to bridge the divide between the 'political left' and 'social left'. Elaborating on the distinction between 'assertiveness' and 'receptiveness' referred to earlier, Sennett points to two leading figures from the past who worked to change the lives of the poor and powerless in Chicago, the city in which Sennett himself grew up – Jane Addams, the pioneer settlement worker and founder of the famous Hull House, and Saul Alinsky, who Sennett describes as probably the most effective American community organizer of the last century. Of the former, Sennett (2012) says

> Addams responded to the problems of difference and participation in a stunningly simple way: she focused on everyday experience – parenting, schooling, shopping. Ordinary experience, not policy formulas, is what counts she thought, in social relations. In this she foreshadowed Saul Alinsky; the test of joint action should be its concrete effect on daily life, not an eventual effect such as policy promises (2012, p. 52).

Of Alinsky and his methods, in particular the role of the community organizer and the receptiveness necessary to understand the issues that affect people in gaining trust as the precursor to animating local communities, Sennett says,

> The community organizer had, and has, to engage poor people who feel paralysed, whether as foreigners or simply losers in the capitalist game. To rouse people from passivity, the organizer has to focus on immediate experience, rather than dramatising, say, the evils of capitalism; that big picture is likely to root even more deeply someone's sense that it is hopeless to get involved (Sennett, 2012, p. 53).

If new forms of co-operation and politics are to be developed on a broader scale, then those on the left will have to take more seriously everyday experience and the importance of locality, community and faith. But it is not just the Left that needs to re-orientate and think anew. Such a process also needs to take place within many of the institutions that make up civil society itself. The assumption that civility resides most conspicuously in the so-called 'Third' or 'civil society' sector needs to be tested and held up to scrutiny. Evers (2010) argues against civility and civicness being accorded a privileged link with a so-called 'civil society' sector. He says:

> It is not – as often assumed – exclusively related to the multitude of associations in society. Such a notion – as one of the most famous theoreticians of civil society Jean L. Cohen (1999) has rightly remarked – is seriously flawed since it leaves out the constitutive role of the public sphere....... The thesis is that associations learn about civility and respect for it by the fact that they operate in such a sphere; it is a forum wherein they have to legitimate their actions. (Evers 2010, p. 114)

If the market and the state are to be held to account and the boundaries of civility and democracy extended then more civil society institutions, including faith groups, charities, community groups and NGOs etc. will need to recognise that the animation of the values they profess necessitates the building of power and political engagement in the public sphere and the inevitable tension that such engagement brings. Ed Chambers, who succeeded Alinsky as Director of the IAF in 1972, talks about the tension between 'the world as it is' and 'the world as it should be'. He says,

> . . it is the fate of human beings to exist in-between the world as it is and the world as it should be. Reflective people of conscience are constantly and painfully aware of the

> gap between our so-called values and the facts of life in the everyday world within which we operate ... The tension between the two worlds is the root of radical action for justice and democracy. (Chambers 2003, p. 29)

CONCLUSION

The state–market nexus which advanced neo-liberal forms of capitalism throughout much of the world in recent decades remains inextricably bound, not least by the massive bail-out of the financial sector that states and their citizens have underwritten. According to Harvey (2010, p. 11), 'Current policies propose to exit this crisis with a further consolidation and centralisation of capitalist class power'. Given such a bleak outlook there is a danger for the current context to be viewed in fatalistic terms in which citizens are seen as powerless pawns in a zero-sum power game structurally determined by the market and state. Against this background an alternative political imaginary is required, bringing together the interests of progressives on the left and civil society to contest the power of the market and to challenge the state when its alignment to the market is to the detriment of the common good of society, particularly the interests of the poor.

Community organising, it is argued, can provide a vehicle for advancing democratic agency by bringing together a broad coalition of institutions from the Left and civil society to contest market and state power. Community organising provides a means to build power and political engagement in localities but also at a broader level, across cities and regions. The success of London Citizens has shown that a power base can be built which provides a platform for people in their localities and institutions to build a political agenda and contest the public sphere. The challenge over the next decade and beyond is to build similar broad-based alliances across other cities and regions in the United Kingdom. In this way a progressive and radical democratic politics can be advanced to challenge existing relations of power and the corrosive effects of neo-liberal hegemony.

REFERENCES

Alexander, J. C. (2006). *The Civil sphere*. Oxford: Oxford University Press.

Alinsky, S. (1989). *Reveille for radicals*. New York, NY: Vintage Books.

Bunyan, P. (2010). Broad-based organizing in the UK: Reasserting the centrality of political activity in community development. *Community Development Journal*, *45*(1), 111–127.

Bunyan, P. (2013). Partnership, the big society and community organizing: between romanticizing, problematizing and politicizing community. *Community Development Journal*, *48*(1), 119–133.

Chambers, E. (2003). *Roots for radicals*. New York, NY: The Continuum International Publishing Group Ltd.

Cohen, J. L. (1999). American civil society talk. In R. Fullinwider (Ed.), *Civil society, democracy and civic renewal*. Lanham, MD: Rowman and Littlefield Publishers.

Davis, R. (2011). *Tangled up in blue: Blue labour and the struggle for labour's soul*. London: Ruskin Publishing Ltd.

Evers. (2010). Observations on incivility: Blind spots in third sector research and policy. *Voluntary Sector Review*, *1*, 113–17.

Garrett, P. M. (2009). *Transforming children's services: Social work, neoliberalism and the 'modern' world*. Maidenhead: Open University Press.

Glasman, M. (2010). Society not State: The challenge of the Big Society. *Public Policy Research*, *17*(2), 59–63.

Harvey, D. (2005). *A Brief History of neoliberalism*. Oxford: Oxford University Press.

Harvey, D. (2010). *The Enigma of Capital: And the Crises of Capitalism*. London: Profile Books Ltd.

Laclau, E., & Mouffe, C. (2001). *Hegemony and socialist strategy: Towards a radical Democratic Politics* (2nd ed.). London: Verso.

Miller, M (2010). Alinsky for the left: The politics of community organising. *Dissent*. Retrieved from www.dissentmagazine.org/issue/winter-2010. Accessed on 26 April 2013.

Powell, F. (2007). *The Politics of civil society: Neoliberalism or Social Left*. Bristol: The Policy Press.

Sennett, R. (2011). A Creditable Left. *The Nation*, (August), 24–26.

Sennett, R. (2012). *Together: The Rituals, pleasures and politics of cooperation*. London: Penguin Books Ltd.

PART THREE

REVIEW AND REFLECTION

As part of interest in and commitment to critical self-reflection we wanted to include an essay which situated this process in the context of conceptual models of learning and thinking with models too of enquiry. The essay included here and our conclusion attempt to contribute to these debates.

Both approaches seek to draw out what and how we might inform our practice and policy choices from an explicit model of learning and reflection. We think that the current on-going crisis across global institutions as well as professional and policy networks underlines the necessity for a systematic review of the relationships between policy decision-making; political choices; institutions and frameworks of governance and the extent to which such approaches promote participatory decision-making. We developed this series to encourage a different kind of conversation between researchers, activists, practitioners and policy-makers. We think that the crises (while they may appear to stabilise) remain and represent an on-going challenge to existing (and known) systems of governance and decision-making.

We think that this represents a challenge too for those institutions (universities in particular but professional administration networks and political networks too – like those that bring together civic leaders) and those engaged with applied research as well as on-going professional development. We think that we need to work with those emerging leaders and networks within civil society too. This represents a major challenge and we would welcome an analysis and critical reflection of what has been achieved so far.

'THE WAY WE DO THINGS AROUND HERE': PERSONAL AND EPISTEMOLOGICAL REFLECTIONS OF THE INFLUENCE OF INTER-DISCIPLINARY IDENTITY ON EFFECTIVE KNOWLEDGE LEADERSHIP FOR TACKLING INEQUALITIES

Alyson Nicholds

ABSTRACT

Purpose – *This chapter seeks to examine the ways in which university-based researchers can facilitate the understanding and awareness of public policy-makers and key decision-makers in the contribution to theory and complexity research can make to contemporary public policy.*

Design – *The chapter provides a systematic literature review informed by reference to key urban regeneration strategies in the United Kingdom.*

Looking for Consensus?: Civil Society, Social Movements and Crises for Public Management
Critical Perspectives on International Public Sector Management, Volume 2, 141–160

ISSN: 2045-7944/doi:10.1108/S2045-7944(2013)0000002011

Findings – *The chapter argues that it is through the promotion of inter-disciplinary approaches to understanding and learning that we might develop the reflective capacities of decision-makers.*

Implications/Originality – *The chapter is intentionally speculative and seeks to encourage critical self-reflection.*

Keywords: Inter-disciplinary; leadership; multi-disciplinary; reflection; reflexivity

INTRODUCTION

As governments strive to come to terms with the effects of the global crisis, public management scholars need to concern themselves with better ways of understanding and theorising some of the complexities which arise. In the face of unprecedented cuts to public services across Europe, a central question concerns how to address growing social and economic inequalities when the austerity measures brought in to avoid further collapse seemingly prevent service providers from going much beyond core services (Birmingham Shared Strategic Assessment, 2012). Effective knowledge leadership between partners lies at the heart of such sustainable development (ESPON, 2012). This is typified in what might be termed a paradigmatic shift away from a Post Fordist economy towards a service-led economy in which knowledge rather than goods become paramount (Surinach & Morena, 2012). But despite acknowledgement of the need to operate differently in this so-called knowledge economy, and much continued effort in the way of physical, economic and social regeneration to re-dress such inequality, we still know surprisingly little about what works to tackle deprivation in such complex times. How can we overcome this notion that traditional policy approaches have continually failed to deliver the goods (Head, 2008); and how, in the face of this, can we create an intersection of knowledge which assists in spanning this inter-disciplinary disconnect (Shergold, 2011)?

Personal and epistemological reflexivity forms the basis for such rigorous and ethical enquiry into such leadership research (Mabey & Finch-Lees 2008, Willig 2001). This implies that there are important choices to be made, not only about what to research, but about the way in which research is designed and the type of data collected (Hackman & Wageman, 2007). Such questions highlight the importance of matters of ontology (how social reality is known), epistemology (how reality is known) and how data is to be collected (methodology) in problematising long-standing policy problems such as poverty and inequality and yet so often these matters remain rather implicit rather than upmost in the minds of those designing such research. But such considerations have the power to either surface or subvert issues, depending on the epistemological lens used. For instance, in leadership development, Mabey and Finch Lees (2008, p. 4) make the important point that no approach is free from value judgements about its moral or ethical stance, and as such can be used as a tool to 'emancipate and release talent on the one hand, but also as a means to control and suppress difference on the other'. This chapter seeks to demonstrate the way that such matters of ontology and epistemology might serve to influence the types of decisions that are made in research into inequalities by drawing on critical research at doctoral level about the outcomes of regeneration. In doing so it seeks to explore the important role that reflexivity and inter-disciplinarity might play in helping to surface some of the prior assumptions held by different disciplines about the root causes of poverty and inequality.

The chapter begins by drawing on personal reflections about the contribution that professional training and background makes to first developing assumptions. In my own case, as a past practitioner of health and regeneration (initially as a nurse and then public health officer) the opportunity to undertake doctoral research to examine the root causes of deprivation represented the pinnacle of a long-standing personal and professional interest in social inequality. But it was subsequently a dissatisfaction with functionalist explanations of such inequalities that later led me to consider the problem through an alternative epistemological lense, including social constructivism and critical theory. By reflecting on both the inter-disciplinary and theoretically diverse nature of my enquiry, this chapter offers both a personal and an epistemological reflection of some of the decisions that were taken in designing research into inequality and how this came to affect the types of evidence that was eventually surfaced in subsequent data.

There are several important reasons for undertaking such an enquiry – academic navel gazing is not one of them. Perhaps of most use is the acknowledgement of both the supportive and critical networks available through peer review and how this might be incorporated into the context of helping others to conduct similar inter-disciplinary research in the future (Allardt 1999). Also of relevance are debates about the value of different types of knowledge that exist in practice (ostensibly in terms of lay public, practitioner, policy-maker and academic knowledge) and the degree to which each is given adequate voice in the process of research. This has a particular relevance in the case of tackling complex policy problems that have repeatedly failed because of a lack of human voice (as with sense-making approaches) or the lack of agency (as with more critical approaches), to which we shall return later. Based on such reflection, the chapter goes on to argue that without such personal and epistemological reflexivity in the research process it is impossible to get to the heart of understanding why policy to tackle inequality might repeatedly fail or how we can begin to address such circularity in policy. The section which follows provides some background to the problem of inequality by examining how it has been written about and understood from three different disciplinary perspectives: the health sciences, the policy sciences and critical geography. On the argued basis that different disciplines have a tendency to view the problem through different epistemological lenses, the chapter goes on to explore the contribution that greater reflexivity can bring to understanding complex policy problems such as tackling inequality using my own doctoral research examining the reasons for ambiguity in urban policy outcomes (Nicholds, 2011).

REFLEXIVITY, INTER-DISCIPLINARITY AND POLICY TO TACKLE INEQUALITY

Often when we think about reflecting on the research process, we tend to think about reviewing and assessing the quality of the data collected or perhaps our own influence on the research process in terms of any pre-conceptions we might have about the topic of enquiry (Denzin & Lincoln, 1998, Marshall & Rossman, 1995; May, 2001). Such reflection has its roots in counselling and psychotherapy with the aim of developing self-awareness (Wolfe 2003). But reflection in the context of research is more about using self-awareness for the purposes of learning and in this sense is more akin to reflexivity than reflection (Carolan, 2003; Giddens, 1976). Indeed, May (2001) goes on to highlight the value of using research diaries in fieldwork as a means of assisting in this process of critical reflection, the main basis of which is to identify areas of potential bias, where the effect of the researcher would otherwise influence the data that is gathered. Thus, we can think of personal reflexivity as involving an assessment of the researcher on the process of research (Horsburgh, 2003).

The idea that different disciplines might have a tendency to view problems differently has long been the study of the policy sciences. This argument posits that professional groups develop their own professional identity through beliefs and values which serve to shape the way that they practice (Yanow 1996, 2000). For instance, Robinson and Cottrell (2005) shows how health care professionals can work together better in multi-disciplinary and multi-agency teams. But we can also speak of a very different kind of disciplinary divide associated with the evidence base from which these different academic disciplines draw their evidence. Such epistemological reflexivity pertains to a different types of awareness associated with the type of data being generated as a result of the ontological and epistemological basis of enquiry, as Dowling (2006) describes below:

> A broader view of reflexivity is evident in epistemological reflexivity where the researcher is required to ask such questions as: 'how has the research question defined and limited what can be found and how could the research be question have been investigated differently?' (Dowling 2006, p. 11)

Building on this, Denzin and Lincoln (1998, p. 2) usefully talk about the idea of the 'researcher as bricoleur' where the research process is viewed as a process of puzzlement in which no single method or discipline is promoted, but rather the researcher is seen as a 'jack of all trades' who is able to access knowledge from across a range of disciplines and who draws on multiple paradigms including Marxism, constructivism and feminism in trying to understand the problem. The idea that disciplines might differ in their understanding of the nature of social phenomena links back to historical debates between the natural sciences and social science. In his discussion of the future of the social sciences in the 21st century, Allardt (1999, p. 15) describes the attempts to 'open up the social sciences' after the second world war after acknowledgement that the worlds' problems consist of social, economic and political dimensions which cannot be separated through the study of single disciplines, such as economics, politics and sociology. For instance, Humphrey and Miller et al. (2012) discuss the limited degree of cross-disciplinary learning in accounting studies. In keeping with this, Raadschelders (2010) notes the value of broad disciplines such as Public Administration which offer a useful medium for studying knowledge integration as by its very nature it is inter-disciplinary. Such debates prompt the question about how different disciplines might have treated different societal problems differently. For instance, how might such inter-disciplinary divides have affected the study and research of inequality? On the basis of personal and epistemological reflexivity, what can we learn about better ways of tackling inequality from bridging the different disciplines of public health, policy science and urban geography? Policy reviews of the literature on tackling deprivation tell us that the continued dedication by governments over more than half a century to designing policy that effectively tackles the root causes of deprivation has resulted in the instigation of a whole range of physical, social and economic approaches through regeneration (Atkinson & Moon, 1994). In the United Kingdom such approaches have ranged from the infamous post-Second World War slum clearances in the late 1950s to the well-documented Community Development Projects in the 1960s through to the economic revitalisation policies in the 1970s, subsequently extended by successive Labour and Liberal-Conservative governments through so-called Third Way policies which seek to combine an economic approach with a degree of social justice (Bunyan, 2012). However, repeated evidence of the so-called unintended consequences associated with health, employment and social inclusion has left many critics asking 'why won't urban policy go away?' (Mossberger & Stoker, 1997). Debate about the likely reasons for the persistent failure of such policy to tackle the root causes of deprivation has long spanned the disciplines of health and policy sciences, each offering their own explanations for repeated failure. But what is it about these different disciplines that lead to such a huge variance in explanation about the nature and cause of inequality? What can be done to create more of an intersection to assist in bridging this divide for the benefit of greater unity in response in the face of global crisis?

In the next section, and by means of an introduction, an attempt is made to examine the ontological and epistemological bases of claims about policy failure to tackle deprivation from three disciplinary perspectives: the health sciences, policy sciences and urban geography. Here, claims are made that the conceptual confusion that exists in the health sciences about the nature and causes of inequality is due to overly rational claims which ignore the human voice (Stone, 2002). Then, by drawing on literature in the policy sciences, the contribution that sense-making can bring to the understanding of inequality as a rhetorical device or metaphor is examined. Based on critiques about the failure of social constructivist perspectives such as sense-making, to account for the socio-political context in which discourse is produced, an alternative perspective is offered, drawing on critical geography literature to consider the contradictory nature of inequality as a form of discursive lack. Following this review of the health and policy science literature, the chapter moves on to draw evidence from my own Doctoral research with a view to being both personally and epistemologically reflexive about the contribution that these different disciplines have brought to my own understanding of policy failure and how we might go about adopting a more inter-disciplinary approach to tackling inequalities in the future.

THE HEALTH SCIENCES: INEQUALITY AS CONCEPTUAL CONFUSION

Much of the evidence about tackling deprivation in the health sciences literature derives from a concern about the nature and cause of deprivation from the perspective of tackling social inequality at the same time as claims of a conceptual confusion concerning differences in meaning. Such inequality can be broadly taken to mean a difference in relation to the rest of the population to the types of resources, services and systems which others may take for granted and the idea that such inequality exposes individuals to a greater risk of death and disease (Navarro, 2009). We can observe the impact of such inequality through reported differences in mortality rates between wealthy and less wealthy areas where, for instance 'in Glasgow, an unskilled, working class person will have a life-span 28 years shorter than a business man in the top income bracket in Scotland' (Navarro, 2009). However, an over-focus in policy on dealing with individual lifestyle at the expense of the less talked about 'wider social determinants' (such as social gradient) has left health policy accused of being tokenistic in tackling social inequality (Graham & Kelly, 2004). Consequently much of the concern in the health sciences literature about the causes and nature of inequality can be linked to a lack of agreement about the meaning of deprivation (Alcock, 2009; Craig, 2001; Graham & Kelly, 2004; Hunter & Killoran, 2004), a lack of agreement about the causes of deprivation such as the role that place plays (Atkinson & Kintrea, 2001; Kleinman & Whitehead, 1999) and the noticeable lack of a suitable theory of change (Parry, Laburn-Peart, Orford, & Dalton, 2004). Not surprisingly, the conceptual confusion arising out of such work has rendered the evaluation of the impact of initiatives like regeneration on health relatively inconclusive (Thomson, Atkinson, Petticrew, & Kearns, 2006). How indeed can we make sense on such conceptual confusion?

THE POLICY SCIENCES – INEQUALITY AS A METAPHOR

Critics in the policy sciences offer some useful suggestions for the likely cause of such conceptual confusion. They remind us of the overly rational nature of policy which ignores the human values in setting policy goals (Stone, 2002; Yanow, 1996, 2000). They show us how by taking a different epistemological view of the same problem, it is possible to see how different disciplines might have treated the problem of inequality very differently, depending on their ideological view of the nature of social reality. This suggests that when examining what works in policy to tackle deprivation, we cannot avoid engaging in epistemological debates about what constitutes evidence. We can see examples of this when we look at traditional models of decision-making where, in general, policy cycles highlight the rational aspects of decision-making involving a new policy problem coming to the attention of policy-makers before considering various alternatives and putting forward ideas for implementation in the field (John, 1998). But the noticeable absence of the public voice in decision-making has led to criticism about the overly rational nature of policy which lacks a human voice (Hajer & Wagenaar, 2003; Stone, 2002).

Taken from this alternative perspective, the policy sciences highlight the important role that human language and values might play in shaping how policy problems are perceived. Such a view is central to an interpretivist tradition of policy analysis in which actors are seen to attach meanings to social phenomena based on their differing ideological backgrounds (Hajer, 1993; Linder, 1995; Yanow, 1996, 2000). Within this important field of study, there has been much valuable work to show how actors use mental framing devices as heuristic constructs in order to make sense of policy problems such as inequality (Rein & Schon, 1993); how they draw on moral storytelling in deciding a potential course of action (Kaplan, 1993); and how reality can have multiple faces depending on the professional background and training of actors (Linder, 1995). Such 'sense-making' to which it is often referred has served the study of problems like inequality well by surfacing some of the otherwise implicit or hidden aspects of policy – but they have also been criticised for missing the valuable context in which discourse is produced too. This can leave interpretivist explanations subject to critique about its overly descriptive and subjective nature by failing to consider either the institutional or structural context in which such discourse is produced.

CRITICAL GEOGRAPHY: INEQUALITY AS A CONTRADICTION

The power of more critical approaches such as Marxism to explaining some of the more structural reasons for the existence of inequality has long been the preserve of critical geographers such as David Harvey whose classic works have focused on how neo-liberalist political economies such as capitalism have served to reproduce social inequality through its focus on generating wealth for the few at the expense of the many (Harvey, 2006). However, post-modernists question the extent to which these 'structural' ways of viewing the problem remain valid in the face of paradigmatic shifts that have taken place away from bureaucratic to market-based and latterly more network-based ways of organising (Bovaird & Loeffler, 2003). This well-trodden debate, which lies at the heart of concern in political science about how society is governed, highlights the need to consider the importance of context when thinking about problems such as inequality. This debate is extended by proponents of post-structuralist theory who suggest that the meaning of ideologies such as neo-liberalism shift over time depending on the social and political context in which it is being studied (Torfing, 2005). For instance, Laclau and Mouffe (2001) show how the meaning of 'man' in Marxist terms as a member of a property owning class or 'man' is different from the meaning of 'man' in functionalist terms as merely a member of the male population. By adopting this more critical view, we can begin to see how by surfacing the hidden meaning of policy to tackle inequalities, it is not only possible for policy to carry different meanings (as with constructivist perspectives), but also how these meanings can also appear contradictory in the face of shifting patterns of governance (Nicholds, 2011). This increasingly complex context is reflected in the idea of an emerging 'knowledge leadership' in the context of recent moves away from the production and manufacture of physical goods towards a more service-led economy, bringing with it a focus on intellectual capital through knowledge (Surinach & Morena, 2012). From an organisational perspective, Mulholland (2002) summarises the impact of such shifts in ideology through her study of the practices of teamworking in call centres, thereby noting how the work design of teams continues to draw on traditional Japanese style (which highlight productivity and performance goals) at the same time as demanding more collaborative and strategic team working. It is this incompatibility which lends critical geographers such as McCann (2007) to asking how we can seek to fulfill the contradictory goals of achieving economic growth at the same time as improve well-being when the striving of the former clearly has such a detrimental effect on the latter. By understanding inequality in this more contradictory way, it is possible to see how this may have been caused by shifting patterns of governance and how, in the collapse of 'Fordist-style economic institutions and Keynesian-Welfare states' new and more fluid forms of knowledge are emerging to fill the gaps (MacLeod, 2001, p. 169). Perhaps what is more exciting are the possibilities this opens up for re-articulating the meaning of inequality, moving away from circular debates about the meaning of inequality to considering how some of the distinctions that have been created may have been no more than linguistic debates based on how a problem is defined. This is something to which we shall return in the next section through my own personal and epistemological reflections from my own doctoral research into what works in regeneration to tackle deprivation. The aim here is to show how by reflecting on the epistemological basis of my enquiry I saw how my original intention to demonstrate the causes of inequality led from an enquiry in which it was the root causes of inequality that were poorly understood (functionalist) to one in which it appeared that different actors interpreted the problem differently depending on their professional background (constructivist). This switch in epistemological approaches not only led me to consider the value of sense-making approaches on the basis that actors might differ in their ideological beliefs about the causes of the problem[1] but also made me acutely aware of the important contribution that methodological approaches such as discourse can make to the more sophisticated analysis of complex policy problems. However, as we will demonstrate later, it was only through the process of presenting my work externally and writing for publication that I became aware of the limiting nature of my enquiry and the need to consider yet again the problems from another epistemological perspective, drawing on critical theory.

PERSONAL AND EPISTEMOLOGICAL REFLEXIVITY OF THE INFLUENCE OF INTER-DISCIPLINARY IDENTITY ON KNOWLEDGE LEADERSHIP FOR TACKLING INEQUALITIES

By means of an introduction, I begin with a snapshot of the professional training I have undertaken over the last 20 years or so since beginning my

Nurse training in 1991, the basis of which is to review some of the micro- and meso-level theories and models which underpinned my early professional training and which subsequently formed the basis of my epistemological journey to studying inequalities from a more macro perspective. Throughout the process, I attempt to reflect personally on prior learning and the contribution that professional background and experience brought to the way we think about inequality. But what I also attempt to show is how by making a very 'real' contribution to understanding the root causes of a problem, this reflection must not only be personal but epistemological too. Here, I seek to show how by reflecting on the choice of methodological approach it is possible to close off particular lines of enquiry by failing to consider the epistemological basis of one's research.

Personal Reflections on Becoming a Nurse and Health Promoter

Following my own professional training in Nursing and the clinical sciences as part of my undergraduate degree, my initial focus was very much an individual one focusing on patient health from a micro perspective, drawing on functionalist knowledge of the natural sciences in subjects such as anatomy and pathology, physiology, immunology and pharmacology to determine the complex causes of disease. Linked to this was a broader study of the individual within society through the study of psychology and sociology along with an evolving skill in clinical diagnosis, drawing on various medical and social models of nursing care (and the associated professional standards of ethical codes of conduct). This process of early professional training saw the beginnings of an evolving professional identity associated with skills in analysis, clinical reasoning and reflective practice, not to mention a strong moral compass, which has remained with me throughout my career as a clinician and later as practitioner and academic. Indeed, relatively recently I found myself listening to a lecture given by a colleague on the role of affect in conflict management in leadership development and was astounded to realise that the leadership competencies to which he was referring were in fact rooted in the counselling and listening skills that I first learned as a Nurse. My interest in developing this skill at University later led to my volunteering as a listener for nightline at University and Samaritans in the care of individuals facing crisis. But it's fair to say that even though these skills proved invaluable working both as a Nurse (needing to 'tune into' patients' every need), I have continued to use them in my work in community development and latterly in organisational studies including leadership. Despite this, I was shocked to learn the findings of a recent paper on leadership in school nursing (Denehy 2008) which revealed a distinct lack of confidence in school nurses about their leadership identity (in that they did not identify as leaders). This fact alone suggests that personal reflexivity (in terms of the values one develops during early professional training) not only acts as an important driver and determinant in building professional identity but also have an inter-disciplinary value.

My move into health promotion and public health, following postgraduate study in Public Health, introduced (for the first time) the notion of community development and the enduring value base of empowerment and how it can be constituted in both individual as well as broader community terms. As with Nursing, the broader theoretical base of Health Education, Health Promotion and Public Health draw heavily on evidence from the health sciences. This in turn has its roots in medical as well as social models of health, the latter of which reflect more critical theories of empowerment, firmly rooted in Frierian ideas about the politics of knowledge and knowing through critical consciousness raising (Etzioni, 1998). Indeed, it is this end goal to which Health Promotion frequently speaks when it talks about the importance of having a strong 'evidence base' in achieving notions of efficiency, equity and efficacy in policy (Tones & Tilford, 1994). But, again, as with Nursing, it is these classical theories within psychology and sociology to which much of the discipline of health promotion alludes, not only in their attempt to account for individual behaviour in society but also by acting as a moral compass to ensure that community needs remain at the heart of policy to tackle inequalities through explorations of power. This is something which on reflection I notice has since shifted in more recent years, through shifts away from the focus on 'people' and onto the focus of 'place'. Furthermore, not only has the emphasis on the social determinants of health since departed regeneration policy, neither is community development funded by the state. But it was this strong notion of social justice that stayed strong with me throughout my work as a community regeneration practitioner working on a housing estate in early 2000, where community needs were paramount, which led me to become concerned that the social needs of communities were not being met through current policy. Here, by being outposted as a practitioner on the estate and working with partners such as the police, housing and youth work, I was faced with the stark reality of poverty and inequality on a daily basis and what it really meant for communities experiencing deprivation. I was only too aware of the reality of some of the issues mentioned in the literature, not least concerns about poor access to public services and concerns about the spatial concentrations of poverty (Kleinman & Whitehead, 1999) – in my case this played out in terms of my own experience of people who lived just 2 miles from a city centre but who rarely left the housing estate. Further experience as a practitioner highlighted the notion that inequality might be defined differently by different stakeholders. Here, for the first time, I made the interesting observation that while the terms 'poverty' or 'inequality' were not especially familiar to the local populace, they were terms whose meaning frequently changed depending on the agency in question (thus linking us right back to the earlier discussion about a conceptual confusion in defining the problem of inequality). It was this important observation as a practitioner which subsequently formed the basis of my own doctoral enquiry into exploring the different ways of understanding what works in regeneration.

Epistemological Reflections of Designing Research to Examine 'What Works in Regeneration'

Early exploration into the literature on inequality identified both a shared and longstanding concern about the effectiveness of policies to tackle social and economic inequality, but from very different perspectives depending on the discipline. For instance, while the health sciences was replete with contested debate about the meaning and impact of poverty and inequality, the urban geography literature raised concern about the persistent unintended consequences of regeneration on outcomes such as health, work and social inclusion (Atkinson, 2000; Curtis, Cave & Coutts, 2002; Parry et al., 2004; Thomson et al., 2006). But it was the incessant focus on the individual at a micro level within the natural and health sciences coupled with a lack of adequate explanation which left me questioning the value of work to evaluate the impact of regeneration policies on outcomes such as health, without considering any of the reasons why such conceptual confusion might persist. Could this, for instance, be due to a lack of political will associated with a mismatch between governments' formal policy statements as compared with their 'real' intentions? This was to form the basis of an ESRC doctoral research awarded in 2007 which sought to examine alternative explanations for making sense about ambiguity in urban policy outcomes.

This move into the policy sciences saw me learning less about the nature and causes of inequality and more about the role of actors in political decision-making at a meso level about policies seeking to tackle inequality. This in turn highlighted the important role that language can play in the policy process through the study of discourse. However, epistemological reflexivity reminds us that 'the meaning, scope and application of such discourse are relative to the different theoretical systems in which it is embedded' (Connolly, 1993, p. 104). Although I began to realise that my initial interest in tackling inequality was aligned to rather more 'functionalist' explorations of 'what works' (during my public health days), later theoretical endeavours led me down other epistemological paths to consider the idea of 'how actors might make sense of policy intentions differently depending on their professional background and experience. Intellectually rooted in early 19th century European phenomenology' (May, 2001) and idealist ontology, such sense-making draws epistemologically from social constructivism suggesting that actors make sense of the world around them on the basis that we act, have intentions about our actions and interpret others' actions. The discovery of such 'sense-making' approaches move would see my study of inequality bringing matters of ontology to the fore in which I became acutely aware of the importance of epistemological reflexivity in planning ones' methodological approach and how it must involve considerations of the nature of social reality. This shift in both my development as an early career researcher and my thinking for the purposes of my PhD led me down a whole series of methodological paths which eventually shifted my approach yet again, from sense-making to critical theory.

The findings of this sense-making part of the study are beyond the scope of this paper (see Nicholds, 2011) but in line with this more constructivist form of analysis, I duly surfaced three discourses of regeneration in which actors could be seen to describe the problems of tackling deprivation in one of three ways: Neoliberal, Welfarist and Communitarian. This first discourse was strongly reminiscent of past economic approaches to regeneration, essentially neo-liberal in their ideology with the aim of generating inward investment, encouraging investment in learning and skills development and the development of entrepreneurial communities. The second discourse was reminiscent of past area-based approaches to regeneration and reflected public health's primary concern with tackling health inequalities through narrowing the gap in life expectancy. This approach to regeneration was largely Welfarist in ideology seeking to instigate place-based regeneration through lifestyle focused public service improvement, community involvement and public accountability. The third and final discourse reflected a capacity building approach to tackling social inequality through community development. This was very much akin to Communitarian ways of seeing and doing and sought to address matters of social justice by placing a high value on plugging gaps in need not met by the public or private sector.

However, following a presentation to colleagues in my department (and some supportive critique too) I was subsequently introduced to critical theory by a colleague from the Essex school (and subsequently at an ESRC seminar series on policy discourse in Edinburgh). Here, my presentation of a sense-making approach to academics on an aspect of regeneration known as Housing Led Regeneration led some audience members to ask the 'so what' question. What they argued here was that while the surfacing of differences in ideology was interesting in itself, it remained in the realm of the descriptive and the subjective since it did little to contribute to deepening our understanding of the reasons for continuing poverty and inequality. This process of reflection was further driven by feedback from peer-reviewers to a journal submission about this sense-making work which pointed me in the direction of the critical geography literature. The combined effect of this advice and critique from experts in the fields of policy science and urban geography prompted a move away from constructivist explanations of inequality and instead introduced me to post-structuralist explanations which drew on critical theory. Returning to the seminar feedback from the Essex school colleague, their suggestion that I might want to take a look at the process of articulation as a more useful means of exploring some of the 'intentions' of urban policy took me down yet another methodological path drawing on Laclau and Mouffe's (2001) theory of socialist hegemony.

The basis behind Laclau and Mouffe's (2001) theory of hegemony (and the reason why it is such a useful theory in the context of exploring reasons for the persistence of inequality) is because it focuses on the way that 'people learn to understand and accept an unjust social order as being natural and in their own best interests' (Mabey & Finch Lees, 2008, p. 135). Epistemologically, Laclau and Mouffe's (2001) concept of discourse is rooted in an anti-essentialist view of social reality where ideas are said to exist in only temporary form because of the lack of a bureaucratic centre or dominant ideological force (Torfing, 2005). Drawing on Derridan notions of dualism (which invites the possibility for two ideas to co-exist at the same time), it is argued that a contradiction results, which Laclau and Mouffe refer to as discursive 'lack'. What they are suggesting here is that meaning is assigned in the process of brokering between these different ideas through the process of 'articulation'. Unlike social constructivist accounts of reality, post-structuralism then posits the meaning of discourse as opaque and elusive which is steeped in ambiguity. In a second stage of research into the causes of inequality, and by being epistemologically reflexive, I was able to apply a second-level analysis to my data by asking a different set of questions to explore the extent to which any of the discourses I had already surfaced were indicative of such lack. Based on this epistemological shift in understanding, I sought to ask the following questions:

- Where is there lack in the discourse of regeneration actors?
- Where are there tensions and contradictions expressed in actors' discourse?
- Where do actors assign multiple meanings?
- Which signifier acts as a nodal point?

This more critical approach to the analysis of the causes of poverty and inequality resulted in the surfacing of the same three discourses, but each of which were filled with a series of contradictions which described the approach in both positive as well as negative terms. This fitted well with the process of articulation described by Laclau and Mouffe (2001) incumbent in the notion of dualisms, where the same concept can hold two meanings. For instance, in the case of the first discursive community, this meant that at the same time as regaling the successes of inward investment and job creation through physical and economic development, they also spoke of a parallel process involving a lack of progress in these areas because of a lack of investment due to global recession. This particular contradiction extended to similar complaints by the other two discursive communities about a failure to 'narrow the gap' or 'build community capacity' because of a lack of investment and overly bureaucratic processes. A full account of the findings is beyond the scope of this chapter (see Nicholds, 2011); however what emerged here was not only the capacity for policy to hold different meanings but how these might only be expressions of the complex social and political times. For instance, what was apparent was that despite appearing to draw on very different ideological bases in their discourses, in terms of Neo-liberal, Welfarist and Communitarian ideologies, on closer inspection, what was especially clear was how the activities of all three discursive communities were surprisingly market based in their approach, suggesting that what they were actually doing was finding different ways of responding to the same new-right hegemony. In keeping with Laclau and Mouffe's (2001) notion of hegemony, this was highly suggestive of the presence of a new-right hegemony pervading all aspects of regeneration practice, and that actors were 'articulating' their ideas about regeneration using a temporary form of rhetoric. What this suggested was that if the reasons for the persistent failure of policy to tackle inequality were potentially rooted in actors' rhetoric then it might be possible to rearticulate a new meaning for policy, based on a more honest account of what goes wrong across the different discursive communities to negate the goals of policy.

CONCLUSIONS

This chapter has explored the idea that complex policy problems such as inequality can be viewed differently depending on the epistemological lens being adopted and that by being more personally and epistemologically reflexive it is possible to surface very different hidden assumptions about what works to tackle inequality in regeneration policy. By reflecting personally on my nursing and public health experience, in the context of moves towards a better understanding the causes of inequality, what my time in health showed me was the value and importance of starting with individual needs assessment in highlighting the hugely diverse needs of people from often very diverse backgrounds. Since moving into the discipline of Leadership and Management, my interest in epistemological reflexivity has been further strengthened through the use of a multi-discourse approach and work on knowledge leadership. Here, the leadership literature offers a unique insight into practical ways of navigating some of the complexities associated with tackling inequality. Perhaps the most pressing need here is to better understand the nature of knowledge leadership and the yet unexplored role that leadership plays in producing and sharing knowledge. Linked to this, recent teaching on the Doctorate in Business Administration (DBA) programme offered me an invaluable opportunity to return to some of the classical research philosophy literature on ontology and epistemology and with it the chance to reflect further on the choices that we might unwittingly make about methodological approach. Here, I had the pleasure of working with DBA students who were well versed in the ideas underpinning research philosophy and who were also very open to the possibility of different approaches to discourse (after some convincing of course). But it prompted a thought about the value of engaging practitioners and policy-makers in the use of such personal and epistemological reflexivity, with a view to surfacing their own hidden assumptions, and that of the organisations they work in. Based on the evidence within this chapter, this opens up possibilities about the best way to go about this in tackling some of the most entrenched policy problems, like inequalities.

By way of an addendum, there are some downsides to inter-disciplinarity which are worth noting. Namely that by working in this way can present difficulties not only in finding an academic home but also in seeking an audience for ones' scholarship. This implies the need not only to seek out like-minded people who share an interest in interdisciplinary research but also to deliberately seek out those who can offer constructive critique. This is with the aim of gently 'challenging' those deeply rooted cultures where any single discipline (along with its preferred epistemological perspective) continues to dominate.

NOTE

1. See Fischer and Forrester's (1993) classic text for an introduction to sense-making approaches.

REFERENCES

Alcock, P. (2009). *Understanding poverty* (3rd ed.), Basingstoke: Macmillan.

Allardt, E. (1999). The future of the social sciences in the 21st century – a comment. *Current Sociology 47*, 13.

Atkinson, R. (2000). Narratives of policy: The construction of urban problems and regeneration policy in the official discourse of British Government 1968–1998. *Critical Social Policy*, *63*(20), 211–230.

Atkinson, R., & Kintrea, K. (2001). Disentangling area effects: Evidence for deprived and non-neighbourhoods. *Urban Studies*, *38*(12), 2277–2298.

Atkinson, R., & Moon, G. (1994). *Regeneration policy in Britain: The city, the state and the market*. London: Macmillan.

Birmingham Shared Strategic Assessment. (2012, June). Retrieved from http://fairbrum.files.wordpress.com/2012/10/shared-strategic-assessment-june-2012.pdf

Bovaird, T., & Loeffler, E. (2003). Public management & governance (1st ed.), Oxon: Routledge.

Bunyan, P. (2012). Partnership, the Big Society and community organizing: Between romanticizing, problematising and politicizing community. *Community Development Journal 48*(1), 119–133.

Carolan, M. (2003). Reflexivity: A personal journey during data collection. *Nurse Researcher*, *10*(3), 7–14.

Connolly, W. E. (1993). *The terms of political discourse* (3rd ed.), Oxford: Basil Blackwell.

Craig, G. (2001). Social exclusion: Is Labour working? 27 September. *Community Care Online*. Retrieved from http://www.communitycare.co.uk/Articles. Accessed on 2 May 2008.

Curtis, S., Cave, A., & Coutts, A. (2002). *Regeneration and neighbourhood change*. Paper prepared for Health Development Agency Seminar. Queen Mary, University of London. 26 June. Retrieved from www.hda-online.co.uk. Accessed on 2 May 2008.

Denehy, J. (2008). Leadership characteristics. *The Journal of School Nursing*, *24*, 107.

Denzin, N. K., & Lincoln, Y. S. (1998). Introduction: Entering the field of qualitative research. In N. K. Denzin & Y. S. Lincoln (Eds.), *Strategies of qualitative inquiry*. Thousand Oaks, CA: Sage.

Dowling. (2006). Approaches to reflexivity in qualitative design. *Nurse Researcher*, *6*(3), 7–21.

ESPON. (2012). *New evidence on smart, sustainable and inclusive territories*. The European Spatial Planning Observatory, Luxembourg.

Etzioni, A. (1998). *The new golden rule: Community and morality in a democratic society*. New York, NY: Basic Books.

Fischer, F. & Forrester, J. (Eds.) (1993). *The argumentative turn in policy analysis and planning*. Durham: Duke University Press.

Giddens, A. (1976). *New rules of sociological method: A positive critique of interpretative sociologies*. London: Hutchinson.

Graham, H., & Kelly, M. (2004). *Health inequality, concepts, frameworks and policy*. Health Development Agency. Retrieved from www.hda.nhs.uk. Accessed on 8 May 2008.

Hackman, J. R., & Wageman, R. (2007). Asking the right questions about leadership: Discussion and conclusions. *American Psychologist*, *62*(1), 43–47.

Hajer, M. (1993). Discourse coalitions and the institutionalization of practice: The case of acid-rain in Great Britain. In F. Fischer & J. Forrester (Eds.), *The argumentative turn in policy analysis and planning*. Durham: Duke University Press.

Hajer, M., & Wagenaar, H. (2003). *Deliberative policy analysis: Understanding governance in the network society*. Cambridge: Cambridge University Press.

Harvey, D. (2006). *Spaces of global capitalism: Towards a theory of uneven geographical development*. New York, NY: Verso.

Head, B. W. (2008). Three lenses of evidence-based policy. *Australian Journal of Public Administration*, *67*(1), 1–11.

Horsburgh, D. (2003). Evaluation of qualitative research. *Journal of Clinical Nursing*, *12*(2), 307–312.

Humphrey, C., & Miller, P. (2012). Rethinking impact and redefining responsibility: The parameters and coordinates of accounting and public management reforms. *Accounting, Auditing & Accountability Journal*, *25*(2), 295–327.

Hunter, D., & Killoran, A. (2004). *Tackling health inequalities: Turning policy into practice*. Health Development Agency. Retrieved from www.hda.nhs.uk. Accessed on 8 May 2008.

John, P. (1998). *Analysing public policy*. London: Pinter.

Kaplan, T. (1993). Reading policy narratives: Beginnings, middles, and ends. In F. Fischer & J. Forrester (Eds.), *The argumentative turn in policy analysis and planning* (pp. 167–185). Durham: Duke University Press.

Kleinman, M., & Whitehead, C. (1999). Housing and Regeneration: The problem or the solution. *National Institute Economic Review*, *170*(October), 78–86.

Laclau, E., & Mouffe, C. (2001). *Hegemony and socialist strategy: Towards a radical democratic politics* (2nd ed.), London: Verso.

Linder, S. (1995). Contending discourses in the electric and magnetic fields controversy: The social construction of EMF risk as a public problem. *Policy Sciences*, *28*(2), 209–230.

Mabey, C., & Finch-Lees, T. (2008). *Management and leadership development*. London: Sage.

MacLeod, G. (2001). From urban entrepreneurialism to a revanchist city? On the spatial injustices of Galsgow's renaissance. *Antipode*, *34*(3), 602–24.

Marshall, C., & Rossman, G. (1995). *Designing qualitative research* (2nd ed.), London: Sage.

May, T. (2001). *Social research: Issues, methods and process* (3rd ed.), Berkshire: Open University Press.

McCann, E. (2007). Inequality and politics in the creative city-region: Questions of livability and state strategy. *International Journal of Urban and Regional Research, 31*(1), 188–196.

Mossberger, K., & Stoker, G. (1997). Inner city policy in Britain: Why it will not go away. *Urban Affairs Review, 33*(3), 378–402.

Mulholland, K. (2002). Gender, emotional labour and teamworking in a call centre. *Personnel Review, 31*(3), 283–303.

Navarro, V. (2009). What do we mean by social determinants of health. *International Journal of Health Services, 39*(3), 423–441.

Nicholds. (2011). Making sense of urban policy failure in complex times. *Regional Insights, 2*(2), 18–20.

Parry, J., Laburn-Peart, K., Orford, J., & Dalton, S. (2004). Mechanisms by which area based regeneration programmes might impact on community health: A case study of the new deal for communities initiative. *Public Health, 118*, 497–505.

Raadschelders, J. (2010). Identity without boundaries: Public administration's canon(s) of integration. *Administration & Society, 42*, 131.

Rein, M., & Schon, D. (1993). Reframing policy discourse. In F. Fischer & J. Forrester (Eds.), *The argumentative turn in policy analysis and planning*. Durham: Duke University Press.

Robinson, M., & Cottrell, D. (2005). Health professionals in multi-disciplinary and multi-agency teams: Changing professional practice. *Journal Interprofessional Care. 19*(6), 547–560.

Shergold, P. (2011). Seen but not heard. *Australian Literary Review*, 4 May.

Stone, D. (2002). *Policy paradox: The art of political decision making*. London: W. W. Norton.

Suriñach, J., & Morena, R. (Eds.) (2012). Intangible assets and regional economic growth. *Regional Studies, 46*(10), 1277–1281.

Thomson, H., Atkinson., R., Petticrew, M., & Kearns, A. (2006). Do urban regeneration programmes improve public health and reduce health inequalities? A synthesis of evidence from UK policy and practice. *Journal of Epidemiological and Community Health, 60*, 108–115.

Tones, B. K., & Tilford, S. (1994). *Health education: Effectiveness, efficiency and equity*. (2nd ed.) London: Chapman and Hall.

Torfing, J. (2005). Discourse theory: Achievements, arguments and challenges. In D. Howarth & J. Torfing (Eds.), *Discourse theory in European politics: Identity, policy and governance*. Basingstoke: Palgrave Macmillan.

Willig (2001). *Qualitative research in psychology: A practical guide to theory and method*. Buckingham: Open University Press.

Wolfe, B. (2003). Knowing the self: Building a bridge from basic research to clinical practice. *Journal of Psychotherapy Integration, 13*(1), 83–95.

Yanow, D. (1996). *How does a policy mean? Interpreting policy and organizational actions*. Washington, DC: Georgetown University Press.

Yanow, D. (2000). *Conducting interpretive policy analysis*. Qualitative Research Methods Series 47. Thousand Oaks, CA: Sage.

CONCLUSION: POLICY AND PRACTICE IMPLICATIONS

Since the fall of 2008 the global economic and financial systems have undergone a series of crises. These crises – some of which are systemic and structural – are not yet resolved. While there appears to be signs of growth and a reduction in unemployment in the United States, there seems little evidence that Europe has emerged from the crisis. Indeed the possibility of a slowdown in China has increased (rather than decreased) the fragility of the global economic system.

These developments – ongoing and unresolved – are, also, part of a much broader set of crises which might be described as ones which cut across economic institutions, but political and social ones too. The global crisis demonstrated the fragility of the global political institutions and structures too. The International Monetary Fund, the World Bank and the World Trade Organisation represent the considered (and settled) institutional frameworks and structures which were designed to avoid precisely the global meltdown from 2008 onwards. The European crisis illustrates very clearly the claim that these structures (including the European Union and the EuroZone initiative) are vulnerable to a worldwide collapse of confidence.

It is the inter-relationship between these different elements – the global financial crisis and the institutional and structural crisis – that formed the basis of this edited collection. We wanted to explore and to reflect upon different facets and elements of these crises and to explore the different implications they have for civil society, public institutions of leadership and governance and systems of regulation too.

We think that there are three broad observations to make and that each of these have research and public policy implications. First, the nature of the crises suggest that conventional strategies and solutions are unlikely to be appropriate; second, the crises are global and international – the responses in different parts of the world add to the overall uncertainty and fragility of existing structures and institutions; and finally, the social, political and structural consequences are likely to be long-term and profound. We discuss each of these below.

REVISITING THE CONTEXT AND RATIONALE FOR THIS COLLECTION

The original aim of this series was that it would invite (commission) contributions from those who had completed pieces of empirical research, but also to secure informed reflections and observations from those who were prepared to be speculative and challenging. At the same time this series is rooted very clearly within a social science/public policy tradition of critical enquiry and analysis. The series draws upon researchers, activists and policy-makers or practitioners who come from these traditions. We also wanted to ensure that contributions to this series were open to the broader/global nature, both of the crisis and of the policy response.

Finally, we wanted to ensure that in this edition we identified and thought about how different policy responses have impacted (positively or negatively) on the lives of residents and communities as they experience different organisational or institutional initiatives. The relationship between the policy process, practice and implementation remains an important part of this series focus. We see these relationships as an integral part of our commitment to research and critical enquiry.

CONVENTIONAL STRATEGIES ARE UNLIKELY TO BE APPROPRIATE

The nature of the crisis – its scale, reach and durability – indicates the case for developing new structures and institutions to meet the needs of the crises. The extent to which such new reformed institutions will emerge is unclear. The capacity of global organisations to resist reform or regulation is self-evident. What is less clear (it seems to us) is the extent to which conventional responses or approaches are able to command confidence or support from broader civil society organisations.

The response of the IMF, the WTO and the World Bank that they can 'manage' the crises without changing their ways of working has much less credibility now than it did in 2007 or 2008. There is a much broader perception that the bankers and those responsible for regulating their industry (political and financial elites) have still not been held accountable for their actions. These institutional weaknesses and failings can be seen as part of a much broader set of institutional and organisational failings which need to be addressed.

At a social and political level we can reflect on how the global post-World War Two economic and financial architecture has failed to support or to keep up with the highly deregulated financial and banking sectors. Indeed, we can argue that the global regulatory institutions (IMF/World Bank) encouraged and promoted the flexibility and light touch regulation sought by the banking industries.

The consequences of these developments are examined in different chapters by Duncan McTavish and Michael Macaualay and his colleagues. In their different approaches they pose key questions about the nature of the crash and also of the policy response to it. In his chapter Duncan McTavish asks the most important question: 'Who's responsible for the state we're in?' As he argues, part of that answer can be found in the dominance of neo-liberalism as the ideological driving force which has under-pinned many of the changes since 1945. But another part of the response needs to be situated within the parallel but linked policy developments in concepts of accountability and reform of public services across the advanced capitalist economies of Northern Europe and North America. It is in this 'space' where ideological ideas dominate the policy discourse that we can see how institutional or organisational structures were reformed in respect of public services and agencies.

Michael Macaualay and his colleagues focus on a separate but important part of this process of change – the relationship between ideas of standards and accountability through regulatory and ethical frameworks. They analyse different approaches to these and how they might support concepts of governance and accountability.

We think that their commentary and analysis on these questions (drawn in the main from a UK perspective) do set out a potential research agenda. In particular, it seems to us that there is scope for examining the different institutions of governance which set the regulatory frameworks and applying the criteria set out in the chapter above. The extent to which the global institutions of the IMF or the G8/G20 are able to negotiate and agree common frameworks of governance and oversight is unlikely. At the same time, however, it provides a lens through which we might reflect upon the strengths and weaknesses of such models.

The regulatory frameworks are, of course, themselves dependent upon a shared discourse of legal rights and responsibilities and notions of parliamentary oversight. As Duncan McTavish argues (so clearly) in a very profound sense the crisis(es) exposed the very fragile nature of these roles and how dependent they were on the relative autonomy of global elites to conduct business on their terms. Their ability to work around systems and rules as well as processes of accountability raise important questions for further enquiry.

We think that part of such a research agenda includes not just seeking to analyse the failure of decision-making and policy implementation but also cuts across the expectations and assumptions we have about the nature of public administration and public management. Specifically, these crises appear to raise significant questions about the extent to which our educational institutions (universities in particular) are sufficiently engaged with the changing needs and context of public administration/management education and training.

The nature of the economic crisis and its political consequences suggest that there is a major need to revisit our assumptions and expectations about the roles of senior administrators and policy advisers to our transnational political elites. The 2008 economic banking crisis is perhaps a key moment in this process of change and transformation. The second key moment has, we think, been the response to the global movements of social change and unrest.

GLOBAL CRISES

The rise of anti-government movements across Europe, North Africa and the United States should not be seen as, in themselves, unusual. Their significance lies, we think, in the nature of these movements and the policy and governance implications they bring with them.

The protest movements across North Africa and Europe and North America were (and are) different. While in some respects they shared some common features, they came from different social and political traditions and this requires us to be careful about how we make sense of what happened. We need to be cautious about looking for overarching generalisations and, at the same time, we do need to reflect upon the changes which are taking place and the extent to which received assumptions or expectations are in a state of flux.

The complex and (at times) contradictory nature of the anti-banking movements should not surprise us. The social and political responses to the global financial crises are reflected in the diverse movements which have emerged. In North America, Europe and North Africa we can observe movements which might be described as 'progressive' and promoting social and political reform based upon ideas of social justice and equality. At the same time we can observe a response which might be characterised as regressive or reactionary and which wants to limit the power of bankers and politicians and is resistant to ideas of social justice and redistribution.

In the United States the emergence of the Tea Party and the move to the right by the Republican Party were not just a response to the Obama victory in 2008. It represented (in part a well-established US tradition) a coherent anti-tax political movement well rooted in the traditions of anti-government/anti-state politics of the United States. But it nonetheless connected with movements in Europe. The rise of the Far Right in a number of European states was (again in part) a response to the crisis within the EuroZone countries and the profoundly significant austerity measures introduced across a number of European states (Ireland, Italy, Spain, Greece and Portugal).

The Far Right in Europe like the rise of the anti-EU party in the United Kingdom (UKIP) shared the same rejection of the European project – which was seen as being both too liberal (the social policy aspects of the EU – Human Rights) and not regulatory enough (immigration and the movement of people). Despite these contradictions these movements posed (and still pose) a challenge to the underlying ideological and political project which is the EU.

Across North Africa the 'Arab Spring' represented something else. The explicit statement and actions of a much broader set of civil society networks, activists and organisations which combined members who wanted progressive secular social change and those who wanted to promote social and faith based values as the dominant ideology of civil and political (or state) institutions.

These were (and remain) times of significant change. In this edited collection we have contributions from Graeme Chesters (on the broad conceptual mapping of the Occupy Now resistance movement); Paul Bunyan (on the specifics of the ideas and ideology which has informed the Community Organising initiative by the UK Coalition Government since 2010) and Dina Wafa (on the impact of the Arab Spring in 2011 for those directly involved in the education and training of leaders in Egyptian public administration).

As these chapters describe and then reflect upon, we are living in a period of political and social change. At the time of writing (Summer 2013) the crises in Egypt are continuing with the intervention of the Army to remove the elected President. We cannot say that civil society institutions are rooted deeply and are robust to withstand change and disruption. What we are observing is the deeply contested and conflictual nature of the debates and we can expect these explicitly disruptive and violent clashes to accelerate across Europe too. Indeed, the rise of the Far Right movements (in addition to the electoral credibility afforded to the National Front in France) across Europe suggests that the next round of European elections for the European parliament is likely to see the emergence of a stronger anti-EU and anti-progressive political groupings in Brussels.

One of the consequences of the unstable nature of the current political and social context is what appeared to be the emergence of anti-austerity/anti-cuts movements in North America and Europe have been overshadowed by the emergence of a more confrontational and socially disruptive movement for political change which has its roots in the Far Right. Both Paul Bunyan and Graeme Chesters' essays explore the intellectual and social/political dynamics present within the Occupy Now/anti-cuts movements in America and Europe (including the United Kingdom). We think that Chesters' essay provides a rich and fascinating set of reflections and analysis on the nature of these movements.

Across Europe – as he argues – the anti-cuts movements brought together a broad alliance of networks and activists. They included trade unions, social networks, neighbourhood and residents groups, environmental activists and a very broad coalition of not for profit/NGOs who were opposed to the ethics and actions of the bankers as well as committed to an alternative set of progressive social values. More significantly, perhaps, the Occupy Now movement as well as those involved in street demonstrations in Europe brought in many young people who have not been politically active or had worked outside the established civil society networks and parties.

The demographics of these movements are important. As Dina Wafa writes (so eloquently) those who framed the new politics were often made up of those on the outside of mainstream political and civil society institutions. On the one hand these movements bring together quite different sets of expectations or assumptions about what might change but this means that there is an innocence which can be attractive. But it also represents a real set of challenges for established practitioners or policy-makers. How do they respond to these new activists and their new forms of protest? The Occupy Now camps are a useful illustration of these dilemmas for established political and social leaders. They represented not just a physical presence of opposition and challenge but also acting outside the usual ways and forms of protest.

We think that there still remains an incomplete research and practice agenda for those involved in public administration or the management and leadership of cities and institutions. New forms of protest and developing new alliances or coalitions of political resistance to the austerity measures will be matched by new models of leadership and governance. At the same time there will be new forms of monitoring and policing too as state institutions seek to protect the status quo.

We want to draw upon the questions raised in these two different sections or ways of thinking about the crisis in our next section.

LONG-TERM NATURE OF THE CHANGES

We argued, at the start of this collection, that we are living in a period of profound change. We do not think this is another small crisis that will pass. We do think its global consequences are significant and that we are in the process of building or developing new institutional structures or systems. In that sense we think the essays by Simon Pemberton and Alyson Nicholds (in their different ways) offer some interesting insights and observations.

Both draw upon the literature and discourse of regeneration (in the UK context this has a well-established literature). In his essay Simon Pemberton looks at the relationship between setting criteria for recognising positive change and progress at the level of the region or the nation state and analyses the models and approaches of UK national government. We think that his significant contribution to this collection is the extent to which civil and political institutions can establish policy frameworks to achieve declared objectives. As he points out there are shared objectives and assumed set of shared ways of working.

Alyson Nicholds draws upon her research into the practice of urban regeneration in the United Kingdom to explore the relationship between the research questions we ask (as well as the policy questions) and the expectations or assumptions we bring as practitioners or policy-makers to our work. The essay is critically reflective on her own work but also provides an important space to think about the underlying assumptions we have as researchers or policy analysts.

Both of these essays add a different set of questions or raise further points of reflection and analysis over a longer time frame. In this collection we have been able to bring together quite different researchers and practitioners from very different perspectives. We have drawn upon their insights and observations and we think that their collective sense of what is happening offers a way into framing the broader questions raised by the Age of

Austerity. The scale and depth of change is profound. The political instability across a number of nation states and within a number of global institutions is evident. We think that new models and forms of leadership will emerge from within existing structures and from across broader civil society networks. We are, however, less optimistic about the short-term than we were 12 months ago.

As with the first volume in this series we do welcome comments and responses. We are happy to engage in a broader conversation.